THEOLOGY
AND ETHICS
OF BEHAVIOR
MODIFICATION

Clyde J. Steckel

University Press
of America™

Library of Congress Catalog Card Number: 79-62910

TABLE OF CONTENTS

PREFACE

The importance of a theological and ethical analysis of behavior modification is argued throughout the chapters of this book. Here in the preface I do not want to summarize that argument. But I do want to set forth my more personal reasons for undertaking this project.

In one sense, it all began with the publication of B. F. Skinner's *Beyond Freedom and Dignity* in 1971. I was at first amused and then amazed at the amount of negative critical comment on Skinner's book. I began to collect as many of the reviews and critical essays as I could find, eventually shaping much of that material into an essay, "The Adequacy of the Behavioral Model," which I presented at the 1973 annual meeting of the Society for the Scientific Study of Religion, and which was later published in *Theological Markings*. It was the work on that essay, along with suggestions from professional colleagues, that persuaded me to undertake a more thorough, book-length study of the theological and ethical issues raised by behavior modification.

But there are personal reasons for this project which go back many years before the appearance of *Beyond Freedom and Dignity*. As a theologian with a dual disciplinary background in psychology, I have espoused preferences (common to such pastoral counselors and pastoral psychologists) for the kind of psychology which seemed philosophically compatible with Christian thought and humane values, broadly speaking, a kind of neo-Freudian, Rogerian, existentialist and humanistic psychology. Conditioning and behaviorist psychologies, in contrast, have always seemed to contain an unwarranted reduction of distinctively human characteristics to stimulus-response mechanisms.

This division between "good" and "bad" psychologies was given its first stern test by Professor Eleanor Miller at Illinois College, where I taught in the religion department. It was a small college, and she was the psychology department. Fresh from my graduate studies, I was enthusiastic about promoting interdisciplinary studies, so I proposed to her a joint seminar in psychology and religion. She admonished me to recall the truly scientific character of psychology and to acknowledge the imprecise and philosophical characteristics of the kind of psychology which I represented. The proposed seminar was eventually held (I trust to our mutual benefit; I know it was to mine). From it, and from my continuing association with Dr. Miller, I was persuaded to make my first major reassessment of behaviorist psychology. While I could not accept its claims to be a comprehensively adequate science, I was more ready than before to affirm its limited but important usefulness in understanding predictable human response patterns.

My second major reassessment of behaviorist psychology occurred during my years as a campus minister at the University of Minnesota.

ii

I discovered once again, in my occasional interdisciplinary overtures, that the behaviorist viewpoint not only prevailed in the department of psychology, but also in education, educational psychology, counseling psychology, and wherever else a fundamental psychological theory informed research and teaching. Eventually I came to know individual professors and gradute students well enough to discover that other theoretical orientations were represented as well. But the overwhelming predominance of behaviorism at the University forced me to reconsider once again my earlier rejection of that whole perspective.

So with these preparatory experiences, I was drawn to consider not only the merits of Skinner's work, when *Beyond Freedom and Dignity* was published, but also to undertake the more comprehensive theological and ethical analysis of behavior modification contained in the pages of this book.

Before proceeding, however, some further personal words of acknowledgement and appreciation are in order:

First of all, heartfelt thanks to my colleagues on the faculty of United Theological Seminary of the Twin Cities, and particularly to Professor Patricia Wilson-Kastner, for criticisms and suggestions on early drafts of the theological chapter.

Secondly, appreciation to Harriet Kruse and other staff members of the United Theological Seminary Library, and to the staff of the University of Minnesota Library system, for their invaluable assistance in obtaining needed books and articles.

Thirdly, much, much gratitude to Marian Hoeft of the United Seminary staff, for her patient and faithful preparation of the final manuscript copy, and Mary Ann Murray, also of the Seminary staff, for her editorial assistance and preparation of the index.

And finally, to the following publishers for permission to quote from copyrighted materials:

Adam and Charles Black Publishers of London, for permission to quote from *The Freedom of the Will*, by Austin Farrer.

The editor and publisher of *Behaviorism*, for permission to quote from "Toward a Constructional Approach to Social Problems," by Israel Goldiamond, in the Spring, 1974 issue.

The Catholic University Press of America, for permission to quote from the *Fathers of the Church* series.

The article by Gardner C. Quarton, reproduced by permission of *Daedalus*, Journal of the American Academy of Arts and Sciences, Boston, Massachusetts, "Toward the Year 2000: Work in Progress," Summer, 1967.

and from *Beyond Freedom and Dignity* by B. F. Skinner, published in 1971.

Research Press, for permission to quote from *Issues in Evaluating Behavior Modification Proceedings of the First Drake Conference on Professional Issues in Behavior Analysis, 1974*, edited by W. Scott Wood.

From *Ethics of Manipulation* by Bernard Häring. Copyright © 1975 by Bernard Häring, used by permission of The Seabury Press.

The University of Chicago Press, for permission to quote from *Behaviorism and Phenomenology*, ed. T. W. Wann, published in 1964.

The University of Minnesota Press, for permission to quote from *Minnesota Studies in the Philosophy of Science*, Vol. II, ed. Herbert Feigl, Michael Scriven and Grover Maxwell, published in 1958.

Yale University Press, for permission to quote from *Freedom of the Will* by Jonathan Edwards, ed. Paul Ramsey, published in 1937.

CHAPTER I: INTRODUCTION

Behavior modification occasionally attracts public attention in dramatic ways. An article or book is published which describes some new "behavioral" method for improving one of those painful and unyielding human problems like mental illness, retardation, crime or delinquency. Or there is an exposé of the dehumanizing and frightening possibilities inherent in some program or ideology of behavior control.

In spite of these occasional periods of public awareness, many people who generally regard themselves as concerned and well informed have only a vague idea of what behavior modification means. This confusion is not altogether their own fault. The term, "Behavior Modification," is used to refer to such widely differing procedures as physical punishment and torture, electrical or chemical stimulation of the brain or nervous system, brainwashing, new methods of psychological counseling and psychotherapy, new methods of treatment for severely retarded or mentally disturbed persons in institutions, new methods of public school education, and fictionalized Utopias describing some imaginary human society in which there is total control and total happiness. Some of these possibilities are indeed frightening, and evoke strongly negative emotional reactions. But some are promising, because they point to better ways to treat intractable human problems.

This book is written for several kinds of readers: First, people like those I've been describing, who know something about behavior modification through magazine articles, newspaper articles, or reports they have heard on the radio or seen on television, and who are both repelled and attracted. I will be trying to make the case that determining appropriate uses of behavior modification in a complex society requires a degree of public information and discrimination which goes beyond such vague knowledge and largely emotional reactions. I hope that this book will assist such persons in gaining a better understanding of behavior modification, and a clearer sense of the underlying moral issues involved in deciding which public policies ought to govern the uses of behavior modification.

Secondly, I am writing specifically for the concerned Christian lay person, pastor, theological student and teacher. I am convinced that behavior modification constitutes one of the pressing public policy issues of our time, on which the Christian community needs to engage in informed theological and ethical reflection, so that the whole Christian community can work toward a social order in which behavior modification is employed in the cause of human well-being. It is also important for the churches to decide how behavior modification might be used within the churches themselves.

While behavior modification may not come to public attention with the force or the persistence of other social problems - hunger, poverty, energy, race and the like - it does surface in a variety of guises, and I want to try to show, in the rest of this chapter, how the question of behavior modification is raised, and why it is an important question for persons of humane and Christian consciences. We will survey two kinds of examples: Behavior Modification viewed with alarm, and Behavior Modification as the solution.

A. BEHAVIOR MODIFICATION VIEWED WITH ALARM

1. Behavior Modification as Brain-Washing

Many people still think of brain-washing when they think of behavior modification. In the late 1940's and early 1950's, brain-washing as practiced on American troops in the Korean War by their Chinese captors aroused considerable public concern. The Chinese method for securing "confessions" proved to be much more successful and much less physically painful than the common methods of torture which have been used through human history. By means of carefully planned deprivations, well-timed rewards and punishments, and a more sophisticated analysis of the psychological strengths and weaknesses of the particular prisoner, Chinese brain-washing effectively broke the will or the spirit of many more American captives than had been the case in World II with the Germans or Japanese. As this information became more widely available in the United States, and as studies were undertaken investigating presumed changes in the American character or psychological makeup which might have contributed to the ease of such confessions, people were made aware that scientifically based techniques for controlling the behavior of other persons could be created, threatening individual rights and autonomy.

How did we get from brain-washing to behavior modification? In the late 1960's, psychologists Edgar Schein and James V. McConnell publicly advocated the use of brain-washing techniques for the most difficult prisoners in our prisons. In an article in *Psychology Today* for May, 1970,[1] McConnell argued that constitutional guarantees of rights to prisoners should not be interpreted in ways that would prevent treatments which would promise to diminish the threat of such persons to the well-being of the society.

In *Harper's* magazine of August, 1973,[2] Jessica Mitford, in an article entitled "The Torture Cure," suggested that liberal treatment philosophies in the prison system, which had attempted to rehabilitate prisoners by modifying their personalities, were being replaced by behavior modification methods which focused on deviant behavior rather than the character or personality of the prisoner.

In its March 11, 1974 issue, *Time*[3] magazine carried a report on behavior modification in prisons. The article described programs in Connecticut, Michigan and Iowa, and also described court challenges brought in those states. In an Iowa court decision, it was determined that the use of drugs to induce vomiting constituted cruel and unusal punishment, and thus was unconstitutional. The American Civil Liberties Union supported a suit against a Federal prison project called START (Special Treatment and Rehabilitation Training). The suit claimed that violations of due process and privacy were a part of such behavior modification. *Time* reported that the project had subsequently been given up in the Federal Prisons. *Time* quoted the ACLU estimate that behavior modification was being used in at least twenty states at that time. In discussing these cases, *Time* observed that some behaviorists "seem... to have adopted and end-justifies-the-means philosophy that is inimical to, or ignorant of time-honored American values."[4] The *Time* article added: "If legislators and judges would produce effective guarantees of voluntariness and less physical abuse and 'aggressive' psychological pressure to modify the behavior of non-volunteers, then much of the controversy surrounding behavior mod might well dissipate."[5]

This identification of brain-washing with behavior modification, and public attention to its use with prisoners, has produced, I would suspect, a great deal of the opposition to behavior modification. Even persons who are deeply concerned about the ever-growing rates of crime and violence in our society are repelled by the use of methods of punishment or control which appear to represent a fundamental invasion of the human rights of the prisoner, who is already confined in a coercive institutional setting.

2. *Behavior Modification as Electrical - Chemical Control of the Brain:*

Others who are alarmed about behavior modification think that it has something to do with the electrical or chemical stimulation of the brain or nervous system. The best known experimenter with direct electrical stimulation of the brain and nervous system is Dr. José Delgado, of the Yale University School of Medicine. Delgado's experiments have been reported in the scientific and popular presses in the 1960's and 1970's, with descriptions of how he has been able to modify aggressive behavior in animals and human beings by sending an electronic impulse into a tiny receiver implanted in the brain, which then sends a controlled impulse into the area of the brain or nervous system which in turn controls the behavior under observation. There have been speculations about

-3-

the possible social applications and abuses of this method, speculations which Delgado has attempted to place in perspective: "We are certainly facing ethical, philosophical and practical problems not exempt from risks... theoretically, it would be possible to regulate aggressiveness, productivity or sleep by means of electrodes implanted in the brain, but the feasibility of mass control by brain stimulation is very unlikely."[6] Delgado does not say whether "feasibility" refers to technical or moral limits. It is all too easy, as we shall see, to avoid ethical dilemmas by postponement. Since we can't technically do it now, we won't worry about the social and ethical implications until we can.

Warning against this kind of ethical postponement is Albert Rosenfeld, in his widely read book, *The Second Genesis: The Coming Control Of Life*. Rosenfeld's book deals with genetic control, the possibilities of a prenatal "design" of the embryo, and the control of the brain and nervous system through electrical and psycho-pharmacological procedures. Rosenfeld is not terribly worried about currently existing social and scientific controls. But he is alarmed about what can happen when we combine drugs and programming. "One thing is certain: we do not have too much time to decide. The bulk of the job ought to be done while the controls at hand are still only social and social-scientific, before the large-scale advent of cheap and easy psycho chemicals, streamlined ESB [electronic stimulation of the brain] and people-forming techniques, and a really massive take-over by electronics and computer systems."[7]

Behavior control using electric and chemical brain stimulation is both alarming and enticing. It is indeed frightening to think about a personal life or a social order in which there is a wide-spread use of such methods to achieve "desirable behavior," however that has been determined. It seems to reduce human beings to machines, immensely complex machines, to be sure, but machines nonetheless. All those uniquely human qualities of spontaneity, unpredictableness, and self-determination would be taken away in such a controlled world.

On the other hand, our culture is strongly committed to applied technology. If anything can be done more efficiently through applied technology, we will do it now and ask questions later. And if human suffering can be relieved and people made happier by applied technology, we are attracted to such possibilities rather than to the much more difficult and ambiguous processes of personal or social transformation in which we must all take responsibility for the outcomes. It's better to fire the old engineers and hire new ones than to face the possibility that we have made bad choices.

There may also be a positive moral argument for chemical and electrical methods of control: the procedures are so clearly intrusive that the subject person or group would have to know about it and give consent. Purely psychological methods of control are feared, however, because it is suspected that these methods can be applied to individuals or groups without their knowledge or consent.

3. *Behavior Modification in "Ideal" Societies:*

Behavior modification is also viewed with alarm by those who associate the term with fictional Utopias in which behavior modification techniques have been used to create a totally controlled society. These novels describe what a human society might be like if "scientific" methods of social control were allowed to trample the freedom and rights of individuals. The best known examples are *Brave New World* by Aldous Huxley, and *1984* by George Orwell. Neither of these modern classics is really about the uses or abuses of behavior modification, but in their nightmare worlds of total social control, scientifically advanced forms of behavior control are employed.

A *Clock Work Orange*, by Anthony Burgess (and the film version made by Stanley Kubrick) presents a society in an advanced state of social disintegration accompanied by terror and violence, in which one form of conditioning is employed in an effort to turn a violently criminal young man into a socially responsible citizen. (The young man is forced by his captors to watch films of violence while taking a drug which induces nausea and vomiting, so that eventually violence will sicken him without the aid of the drug). In both its literary and cinematic forms, A *Clock Work Orange* is a chilling social document.

These three novels are warnings. A similar work of fiction published in 1948, *Walden Two* by B. F. Skinner, was not intended to be a warning but a promise. In spite of that intention, however, many readers and critics have also viewed *Walden Two* as an image of a behaviorally controlled future which should be avoided at all costs.

B. F. Skinner is one of the truly distinguished behavioral psychologists of all time, and we will be examining his ideas at many points throughout this book. For now we will look at his ideas about a behaviorally ordered social Utopia as presented in three of his major works: *Walden Two, Science and Human Behavior,* and *Beyond Freedom and Dignity*. These are three quite different books - a Utopian novel, a survey of behavioral psychology, and a prophetic political essay. But the central question is the same: how to create a better social order through the application of scientific psychology on a vast scale.

Walden Two describes the rural New England Utopian community set up by Frazier, a former graduate student at a mythical Eastern University. Professor Burris, a psychologist and the narrator, and Professor Augustine Castle, a philosophy professor at the same institution, take a trip out to see the commune and to talk with Frazier. Most of the book consists of debates on political philosophy among these three men. The philosopher comes out rather badly in these debates. Burris, the psychologist, wavers, but finally succumbs to the attractions of the commune, and the novel ends with Burris forsaking university life to join *Walden Two*.

The same ideas are developed further in *Science and Human Behavior*, published in 1953. In a concluding set of chapters entitled "Controlling Agencies," Skinner analyzes government and the law, religion, psychotherapy, economics and education as examples of behavior control. Skinner then argues that we should be able, with behavioral technology, to design a culture more intentionally and explicitly than has ever been done before. He contends that such a deliberate design of a culture should be undertaken in order to enable culture to survive and grow, rather than suffer the likelihood of extinction, a fate which, Skinner observes, has come to all other cultures in human history.

These same ideas were further elaborated in *Beyond Freedom and Dignity*, published in 1971. While Skinner's advocacy of a behaviorally planned and controlled culture remains substantially the same in this volume as in the other two, Skinner mounts a more direct frontal attack against the cherished notions of human freedom and dignity, and the way in which the belief in freedom and dignity keeps people from considering the merits of a behaviorally designed culture.

His argument runs as follows: the application of science to human affairs has given us, for the first time in human history, the technological means (behavioral psychology) to control human societies in ways which have been largely uncontrolled and unplanned in the past. But we are inhibited from using these new scientific methods of control because of our commitment to ideals like human freedom and dignity. Freedom and dignity were once important, indeed indispensable values in the evolution of human culture from the control of despotic governments and despotic environments. But we are now at a new stage of human history in which our commitment to freedom and dignity has become harmful rather than helpful. Because of our belief in freedom and dignity, we try to produce desirable behavior by punishment or the threat of punishment, and by persuasion. But these are now known to be crude and ineffective methods of human influence. Through the principles of positive reinforcement or operant conditioning (which will be explained more fully in chapter 2) we are now far more effective in eliciting desirable behavior from people, and so we can build a society in which human needs will be met and the greatest human happiness will be achieved.

According to Skinner, we stand at a critical juncture in human history because we can observe an advanced state of cultural decay in Western civilization. Skinner points to the familiar problems -- crime, violence, alienation, boredom and apathy, economic malaise -- as symptoms of the urgency of the crisis. Cultures which survive and grow, he argues, are those in which people are induced to work for the survival of the culture itself. Since we now have the technological means, we should be at work redesigning our culture in such a way that behavioral methods of control will guarantee its continued survival and growth. To do less, he argues, would be to fail the major challenge of our time.

Soon after its publication, *Beyond Freedom and Dignity* was subjected to onslaughts of critical comment in newspapers, magazines, scholarly journals, and on radio and television. Most of it was hostile. The outrage was focused on Skinner's rejection of human freedom and dignity. That Skinner was willing to reject these values for the sake of a certain kind of cultural survival seemed to many critics an unconscionable moral position. Other critics attacked the inflated claims which they thought Skinner made for the capability of behavioral science. Many of these critics were Skinner's professional colleagues in psychology. They argued that while behavioral science had demonstrated the ability to predict and control certain behaviors in human or animal subjects under certain limited conditions, nothing in mass behavioral technology existed or could be foreseen to establish the kind of total social control which Skinner advocated.

There was so much criticism and there were so many debates that Skinner attempted to address his critics in a subsequent volume, *About Behaviorism*, published in 1974. These are disappointing essays, because Skinner simply repeats the arguments in *Beyond Freedom and Dignity*, and does not really address the substance of the opposing arguments. It has been particularly frustrating that Skinner does not appear able to entertain the possibility that human freedom and dignity are morally irreducible values, at the same fundamental level as his own beliefs in science and cultural survival. So long as Skinner continues to assume that survival and science are more fundamental than freedom and dignity, it appears unlikely that this debate can move beyond its presently polarized condition.

For a great many people today, B. F. Skinner's ideas about a benevolently controlled society are among the things that come to mind when they think about behavior modification. If that is what behavior modification is about - a scientifically controlled social order in which freedom and dignity have become obsolete - they want no part of it. It is unfortunate that behavior modification is so closely associated with Skinner's Utopian social philosophy, because attention is diverted from the many ways in which behavior modification is already employed in our society, ways which ought to be better understood and subjected to informed policy review. Instead people are "against" behavior modification because they think of it as a controlling social philosophy.

The examples discussed so far - brain-washing, sophisticated forms of punishment, electrical and chemical stimulation of the nervous system, and fictionalized warnings about a behaviorally controlled society - do indeed suggest alarming possibilities. But this is not the whole story.

B. <u>BEHAVIOR MODIFICATION VIEWED AS THE SOLUTION</u>

We are becoming increasingly aware of positive applications of behavior modification, reported in the same magazines and newspapers carrying the continuing debates over Skinner's brave new world. These uses of behavior modification occur in psychotherapy and psychiatry, education (particularly the education of the mentally retarded, autistic children, and youngsters with severe behavior problems), the treatment of chronic mental illness, and a variety of self improvement programs.

1. *Behavior Modification Psychotherapy:*

In psychotherapy and counseling, a number of new methods based on behavior modification principles have been created, methods which claim to show a dramatically higher rate of cure than is to be found in classical psychoanalysis or psychotherapy, and requiring fewer sessions than typical in long-term psychotherapy. Dr. Joseph Wolpe of Temple University has pioneered one of the best known behavioral therapeutic systems using systematic desensitization. He claims an 85% success rate for his method, requiring fewer than 30 sessions. Wolpe's system is but one of several methods of behavioral counseling which will be examined in greater detail in chapter 2.

2. *Behavior Modification in Education:*

The applications of behavior modification in education which have attracted public notice are varied and dramatic. Ivar Lovaas at UCLA has demonstrated the value of behavior modification in treating autistic children - so severely withdrawn emotionally that existing methods of treatment and education simply could not establish the necessary minimal communication which was required. By using mild but noticeable electric shocks administered in immediate conjunction with undesirable behaviors, Lovaas was able·to demonstrate gains in social skills which were thought to be impossible with such severely disturbed children.

Another widely reported and discussed application of behavior modification in education has been taking place in a black housing project in Kansas City, Juniper Gardens. A group of applied behavioral scientists headed by Donald M. Baer developed a multi-faceted project including pre-school classes for children, a day care center, a recreation center, a reading and tutoring program, and a tenants association, all of them organized around behavior modification principles. Bryant School, also in Kansas City, presents an example of efforts to apply behavior modification through-out a school system.[8]

The *Saturday Review of Education* for April, 1973 carried a report[9] on Montgomery Hill's Junior High School in Silver Springs, Maryland, where behavior modification was being intensively practiced. Such school applications require the maintenance of detailed records of desirable and undesirable behaviors of each child, on the basis of which appropriate reinforcements are devised for eliminating the undesirable behaviors and increasing the desirable ones. At Montgomery Hill's Junior High School, a point system had been devised which enabled students to earn points for good performance and good behavior. These points could then be used to purchase rewards - typically time away from formal class sessions and in an informal school area where refreshments could be obtained.

3. *Behavior Modification in the Treatment of Mental Illness:*

The classical study and demonstration of behavior modification in the treatment of severely disturbed mental patients was conducted by Teodoro Ayllon and Nathan H. Azrin at the Anna State Hospital in southern Illinois. They demonstrated the usefulness of a "token economy" method for inducing positive behavior changes in otherwise severely withdrawn and non-cooperative patients. They showed that psychotic patients who had been in the hospital for a long time could learn how to care for themselves, accomplish certain house-keeping chores, and hold hospital jobs by means of a system in which the patients received the tokens for performing desirable behaviors. These tokens could be then spent for some privilege or reward which was of value to the patient. The key to a success-ful token economy system was a precise analysis of the positive rewards which each individual patient valued, and in what order of priority. This token economy method has now been applied in many kinds of institutions and settings - with retarded children,

slow learners and juvenile delinquents, as well as with adult
psychotic patients in mental hospitals.

4. *Behavior Modification in Self-Help Programs*:

In addition to these widely publicized applications of
behavior modification, there are also articles in magazines
describing applications of behavior modification in a variety of
self-help programs. *RedBook* magazine for August, 1972, carried
an article by Sally Hardcastle entitled, "How to Change Your
Husband's Bad Habits (and how he can change yours)". The article
described a research project conducted at Cornell University in
which ten wives were trained in changing their husband's behavior
using behavior modification methods. Charts were developed in
which the wives kept track of the number and frequency of desirable
and undesirable behaviors, along with identifying the events which
appeared to be linked casually to the behaviors which were being
charted. The article went on to describe a system of marriage
counselling developed by Dr. Mark Goldstein in which husbands
and wives were taught a system for using these charts for each
other, so that they could maximize positive behaviors and habits,
thus displacing negative behaviors and habits. Dr. Goldstein
admitted that it was difficult to be successful using behavior
modification unless the couple were truly committed to each other
and to their marriage. The article concluded with instructions
on how couples might try this charting method at home without
the necessity of professional consultation.

Business Week magazine for June 8, 1974, carried the story
of a pilot project being conducted by the Ford Motor Company for
improving the health of their top executives. Included were
behavior modification techniques for eliminating smoking, controlling diet and diminishing tension.

Psychology Today magazine for April, 1975, carried an
article about the treatment of the behavioral problems of pet
animals using behavior modification methods. Again the key to
successful behavioral management of pet behavior problems was the
keeping of a detailed chart on specific units of pet behavior and
discovering what were the immediately reinforcing events. The
therapists would then advise the pet owner on possible reinforcements which could be employed to extinquish the undesired behavior
or to reinforce a positive behavior which was to take its place.

In the same magazine for November, 1975, an article by
Patrice Horn described procedures which had been developed for
enhancing healthy sexuality by using behavior modification
methods. Combining encounter group methods with behavior modification techniques, the therapist attempted to deal with verbal

inhibitions, fears and hopes, initiation and refusal, specific behaviors which were "turn-ons and turn-offs," and a system for teaching instantaneous communication feed-back.

And an article by Evan Frances in the *Ladies Home Journal* for January of 1976 described a new diet plan using behavior modification, in which specific behavioral strategies are taught in a step-by-step method which will result in a reorientation of eating habits and a consequent loss of weight to reach the desired level.

These are but a few examples of the applications of behavior modification. Such articles appear often enough to create the impression that applied behavior modification may indeed be the solution to some of life's besetting problems. In the current literature on behavior modification for professional readers, the list of applications runs on and on: the management of anxiety, the treatment of depression, applications in the classroom, treating hospitalized persons, applications in medical and nursing practice, behavioral principles in experimental communities, group homes for delinquents, behavior modification in prisons, the treatment of sexual deviations, social skills training, alcohol and drug abuse, the management of obesity, programs to help persons to quit smoking, and the behavioral treatment of marriage problems.[10]

Enthusastic and extravagant claims for behavior modification appear in the professional journals as well as in popular magazine articles. Behavior modification is presented as the solution. Even allowing for these excesses, the results reported are impressive. If behavior modification only does half of what is claimed for it, the advances over existing treatment and educational programs would be staggering.

C. CONCLUSION AND PROSPECTS

How are we to judge, then, whether behavior modification promises important new solutions for human problems or is a cause for alarm? I believe that the answer to this question is to be sought at a deeper level of analysis than we find among the alarmists or the enthusiasts. The alarmists argue that all behavior modification is inherently shallow and manipulative, and if followed out to its philosophical and moral implications, entails the loss of our most deeply held moral and social values. The advocates of behavior modification argue that since behavior modification works ("work" meaning the ability to solve or deal with difficult or insoluble human problems), then it should be used, since the improvements in human achievement gained by its use are well worth any temporary or limited abrogation of what we conventionally understand as human rights.

-11-

These two arguments appear to be irreconcilably opposed. And as long as the arguments are so stated, it is difficult to imagine any reconciliation. I believe that these two sides are not nearly so irreconcilable as the arguments would appear, however, and it is my purpose in this book to show why I not only believe that a degree of reconciliation can be achieved, but also why it is important to do so.

In order to make that case, the remaining chapters of the book are developed in the following way: Chapter 2 contains definitions and some historical background on selected key terms: behaviorism, behavior control, behavior therapy, and behavior modification. Readers with a knowledge of psychology may want to skip this second chapter and go on to the third. But I suspect that many readers will find it helpful to examine these definitions, precisely because of the confusion about the meaning of behavior modification described in this First Chapter.

Chapter 3 deals with the question of the truth of the behavioral orientation. To what extent is it true that human behavior is the predictable and thus controllable product of environmental influences? This question leads inevitably to the free-will-determinism question, which has taxed thinkers for centuries. I suspect that many readers will find this third chapter difficult to grasp. And because I write as a Christian theologian, I must deal with questions of truth in a Christian theological framework. Many readers may find that framework unfamiliar or uncongenial. But I hope that they will bear with this discussion even so. What I have to say in the succeeding chapters about moral issues and applications of behavior modification will be rooted in the discussions contained in the third chapter.

The fourth chapter deals with the moral and public policy questions: Under what circumstances, for whom, and by whom should behavior modification methods be employed? We shall look at examples of the current debates regarding the ethics of behavior modification, and I shall propose principles for making decisions about specific cases.

The fifth and final chapter of this book deals with the specific institution in which I teach and for which I bear personal and professional responsibility - the church. We shall look at ways in which applied behavior modification methods are already employed in the life of the churches, and I will suggest some other areas in which applied behavioral methods might be fruitful. I would hope that general readers who may not be particularly concerned about religious organizations might still find in this chapter some ideas about institutional applications of behavior modification which they will be able to translate into the institutional settings which are the most important to them - the family, the school, business and industry, the neighborhood or community organization.

I do hope that all readers, whether coming from a Christian theological and ethical concern or from the standpoint of citizens concerned about personal and social well-being, will find this book helpful in thinking through the promises and perils of behavior modification. I trust by now it is clear that I believe that both are to be found in behavior modification. If we are successfully to avoid the perils and realize the promises, all of us - Christian and non-Christian alike - will need to find ways to bring informed concern and judgment to bear at those places in our society where professional and institutional decisions are made about research and application in behavior modification. I hope this work contributes to that process.

NOTES FOR CHAPTER I

[1]James V. McConnell, "Criminals Can be Brain-Washed Now," *Psychology Today* (May, 1970), 14-18, 74.

[2]Jessica Mitford, "The Torture Cure," *Harper's Magazine* (August, 1973), 16-30.

[3]*Time* (March 11, 1974), 74-75.

[4]*Ibid.*, 74.

[5]*Ibid.*, 75.

[6]Jeannie Reinert, "Brain Control," *Science Digest* (November, 1969), 17.

[7]Albert Rosenfeld, *The Second Genesis: The Coming Control of Life* (Englewood Cliffs: Prentice-Hall, 1969), 286.

[8]A good description of these projects is contained in an article by Kenneth Goodall, "Shapers at Work," in *Psychology Today* for November, 1972.

[9]Daniel Zuerdling, in *Saturday Review of Education* (April, 1973), 52.

[10]Readers desiring to examine this professional literature should consult the following journals: Journal of Applied Behavior Analysis, Journal of Behavior Therapy and Experimental Psychiatry, Behaviour Research and Therapy, Behavior Therapy, and the Journal of Consulting and Clinical Psychology.

CHAPTER II: DEFINITIONS - BEHAVIORISM, BEHAVIOR CONTROL, BEHAVIOR MODIFICATION, BEHAVIOR THERAPY

In the previous chapter we looked at behavior modification from many sides, without ever attempting a formal definition. In doing so, we discovered that people think of many things as behavior modification - from brain-washing to weight-reduction. Some of these meanings were alarming, some were hopeful. In deciding whether behavior modification should be affirmed or rejected, I argued that alarm or enthusiasm were not sufficient grounds for judgment. We need a more fundamental analysis of the questions involved.

A fundamental analysis requires clearer definitions of key terms than we needed in the previous chapter, where we surveyed what people associated with behavior modification. So we now preceed to the definitions of four key terms: behaviorism, behavior control, behavior modification, and behavior therapy.

It would be tempting to cite several definitions from contemporary texts and then move on, but I fear that such a textbook approach would leave many readers wondering how these definitions were selected and whether they were sound. So I must ask for the reader's patient indulgence while I describe some of the pitfalls to be avoided in constructing definitions.

It is really not the case anyway that definitions simply exist somewhere in a book to be "looked up." Dictionaries, encyclopedias, glossaries and summary statements in textbooks are immensely helpful, of course. But these definitions all represent a complex distilling of past and current usages, and the editors or authors must make interpretive decisions about very complicated questions. The dictionary or encyclopedia approach to definitions necessarily sacrifices complexity, historical dimensions, and subtle shades of meaning in order to arrive at reasonably simple and clear statements.

We can go in the other direction and look for definitions by describing the origins and the history of usage of the term to be defined. This is an appealing approach because it conveys a much fuller and richer sense of meanings, shifts in meanings, and reasons for these changes. But the drawbacks of an historical approach are considerable. It is frequently difficult to trace terms to their origins. The story can become quite lengthy and involved. And the outcome can be considerably less clear and focused.

Or we can simply take the set of definitions proposed by a single authority - B. F. Skinner, Albert Bandura, or whoever. We can expect to gain logical consistency from this approach, but at the sacrifice of breadth and, alas, often at the sacrifice of clarity, especially for the lay reader.

In the definitions that follow, I have attempted to honor what I take to be a working consensus among behavioral psychologists, without aligning myself with a particular faction or leading authority. I have tried to write for the lay reader, not the professional, and I attempt to include enough historical background so that these definitions do not just appear out of the air.

Before proceeding to the first definition, an explanation is in order for selecting just four terms to define, behaviorism, behavior control, behavior modification, and behavior therapy. Why these terms and no others? These, I believe, are the key terms for understanding something about the scholarly disciplines and professional practices to which they refer. And these are the terms which occur most frequently in public discussions and debates regarding the appropriate uses of applied behavioral science. One could go outside this set of terms for the sake of increased scholarly mastery into a whole glossary of specialized terms used in behavioral psychology. For readers interested in learning terms other than those presented here, references will be given at the end of the chapter.[1]

A. BEHAVIORISM

We must define behavior in a book about behavior modification because behavior modification, as a set of procedures, is derived from behaviorism as a theoretical and scientific approach to understanding the behavior of living things.

Behaviorism has two distinguishable but related meanings: Behaviorism is a distinct school of thought in modern psychology; and behaviorism is a more general scientific outlook on the behavior of organisms, an outlook which tends to predominate in the whole field of psychology in the United States.

The history of modern psychology can be told as the story of a discipline which disconnected itself from its historic roots in philosophy and increasingly aligned itself with biology, the laboratory approach, and the rules of investigation and reasoning which broadly characterize modern natural science. This migration took place in the last half of the 19th and the first half of the

20th centuries. In the course of this migration, psychology developed succeeding and often competing schools of thought. Behaviorism was one such school of thought which arose as modern psychology attempted to legitimate its place among the natural sciences. John B. Watson is generally regarded as the founder of behaviorism, though there are clear antecedents which should be noted. One could argue that behaviorism is to be traced all the way back to Renee Descartes, the seventeenth century rationalist philosopher, who held that the human being, in its physical or material properties, was a marvelously complex machine, obeying all of the natural laws which governed the behavior of things having substance. Descartes also believed that the human being was directed by a rational soul or mind. But he found it difficult to specify the ways in which a free mind could direct a machine governed by natural law. This problem continues to be a characteristically modern preoccupation, because science and technology require that we believe in some kind of natural law, from which human beings are not exempt. But the philosophical and moral foundations of our culture require that we believe in freedom and responsibility. This dilemma will be explored more fully in the next chapter.

More recent antecedents to the work of Professor Watson can be found in the laboratory work done in psychology and physiology in the latter decades of the nineteenth century and the early years of the twentieth century. Ivan Pavlov, the Russian physiologist who demonstrated the fact of conditioning and some of the principles of conditioning, is often cited as one of the founders of behaviorism. While Pavlov was not strictly a behaviorist, his work on conditioning-- the ways in which a specific stimulus (the sound of a bell) can be employed to obtain desired responses in an organism (salivation)-- contributed to the formation of the principles of behaviorism.

Watson, who was a psychologist at the University of Chicago and then at John's Hopkins University before finishing his career as a psychologist on the staff of a major advertising agency, published his landmark article in 1913, entitled "Psychology as the Behaviorist Views It." This article was a manifesto, calling for the creation of a truly objective science of psychology. To become a science, Watson argued, psychology must discard all "mentalistic" terms, that is, all terms which attempt to describe what is going on inside the mind of the person or the animal being observed. Previous methods of psychology used reports in which subjects attempted to state what was happening in their minds during the experiment or in the experience being studied. These reports constituted the "data" of psychology prior to Watson, and Watson argued that such reports could never be used to develop a truly objective science. Such a science was methodologically impure. Comparing the reports of different persons on their inner

-17-

thoughts or feelings was not a procedure for verification. It
could not be repeated with other subjects under identical conditions.

What that leaves for a truly scientific psychology, therefore,
is the _behavior_ of the organism - whatever the organism does which
can be observed. Watson believed that there were no such things
as instincts in human beings, and that whatever one might make of
the influence of heredity, the really controlling dynamics for
living organisms were those presented to them in their environments. So psychology was to become the pursuit of the lawful
relationships which are believed to obtain between specific
stimulating events in the environment and the specific actions
or behavior which these events produce in the organism.

There was a refreshing simplicity and clarity about Watson's
psychology. It was a critical turning point for the whole discipline,
because while scientific studies of animal and human behavior had
developed considerable sophistication and complexity during the
early decades of the twentieth century, there was always the haunt-
ing suspicion that the foundation itself might be exceedingly weak,
since research on human beings was based on reports of internal
states of mind or feeling which no one else could examine or verify.
Watson cleared away all of those suspicions, and helped form a
scientific psychology which could claim to honor all the rules of
exact investigation and reasoning which were believed to characterize the other natural sciences. There was, however, some loss
with this gain, since the entire domain of human thought and feeling had to be ruled out of bounds to possible scientific explora-
tion. But that seemed to Watson and his followers a small enough
price to pay for scientific objectivity and respectability.

Following Watson, other psychologists identified themselves
with the behaviorist point of view, and a rich and complex history
of behaviorist research efforts and theoretical debates emerged in
the 1920's and 1930's, including a school which came to be known
as Neo-Behaviorism. The Neo-Behaviorists were characterized by
an emphasis on theories of learning, on combining evolutionary and
"need" theories with classical behaviorism, and "operationism,"
which was the view that the validity of a concept dependent upon
the validity of the operations employed to arrive at the concept.

B. F. Skinner has become a leading exponent of behaviorism
as a school of psychology. A Professor of Psychology at Harvard
University, Skinner continues the traditions of Watsonian behaviorism. Like Watson, Skinner is a radical environmentalist, arguing
that behavior is always causally linked to events in the environment.
Thus all behavior can, in principle, be predicted and controlled.
Skinner's most important theoretical contribution to the refine-

ment of behaviorism has been the discovery of operant conditioning. A pigeon discovers that if it pecks on a particular color or number on a revolving disc, it will receive a pellet of food. So the hungry pigeon quickly learns to operate on its environment in a highly discriminating and effective manner. Or a child discovers that putting away a toy elicits a smile and hug from a parent, and so the child puts away more toys in order to elicit the same response again and again. Much of Skinner's scientific work has been directed to the discovery of the conditions under which such behaviors are initiated, sustained, or extinguished. This is operant conditioning, or operant behaviorism.

While there are other enduring schools of thought in psychology - Freudian, Jungian, existential, humanistic, and the like - behaviorism seems to have lost some of its earlier "school-of-thought" qualities, such as partisanship and reforming zeal. That is probably because behaviorism has become the dominant orientation in psychology departments in colleges and universities. And behaviorism is increasingly the reigning psychological orientation in other social sciences and in the professions like education and social work which depend on the social sciences for scientific grounding.

So we come to a second definition of behaviorism, not just as a school of thought in psychology, but as a more general scientific outlook permeating the social sciences, the social professions and, indeed, popular culture as well. This permeating influence could be documented with examples of behavioral ideas and language which have come into the vocabularies of the social sciences and professions, for example, talking about behaviors rather than actions, or reinforcements instead of rewards. But let me try instead to outline some themes which represent the essence or spirit of the behavioral perspective: 1) a belief that everything, including human experience, exists in predictable patterns of causal regularity. While in a given science or in a specific area of investigation these predictable patterns may not yet be fully known, it is important to believe that there is nothing which in principle lies outside such causality. 2) the belief that whatever constitutes the "uniqueness" of any group of people or of a particular person must finally be understood to be the product of the history of conditioning which that group or person has experienced. Even the most private and personal dimensions of "inward" experience follow these same patterns of predictable regularity. 3) scientific investigation of these causal patterns is the best, indeed is the only fruitful way to obtain the knowledge needed to solve intractable human problems. 4) environmental determinants (including determinations which arise "within" the organism) are the key explanatory factors. What we call wishes, desires, feelings and decisions are really clusters of repeated patterns of environmental determination.

These behaviorist themes, I would argue, are pervasive not only in psychology and the social sciences. They are evident in American society and Western culture as well, not to the exclusion of cherished beliefs in freedom, initiative and responsibility, but as an extremely powerful counterpoint. It is not really so surprising that a culture ideologically committed to freedom should also believe in causality. Science and technology have served us well. Gratitude shapes belief more powerfully than logical consistency.

B. BEHAVIOR CONTROL

Behavior control does not refer to a particular school of thought in psychology nor to a particular set of methods, but to any kind of psychologically based effort to establish control over the behavior of another person or persons. Control is the key word. And there are two kinds of control. First, there is the kind of control which is one of the aims of science - the ability to predict and control future events. All science aims at achieving the kind of knowledge which will enable events to be predicted and thus controlled. If we know how and why something happens, we can then arrange the conditions for it to happen again, if it is positive, or see that it does not happen again, if it is negative. Behavior control simply refers to that kind of scientific precision in the realm of behavior. (It should be noted that while psychology has been endeavoring to assert its rights to predict and control with precision, just like the natural sciences, these natural sciences, like physics, chemistry and biology, have tended increasingly to speak of levels of probability rather than certainty, and to back off from absolute claims to be able to predict or control.)

Behavior control also means another kind of control. It means the deliberately planned effort to control the behavior of another person or group of persons in ways that are judged to be desirable. That judgment may be made by the person or group trying to change its own behavior - the overweight person who wants to control eating or the group of management executives who want to replace their ineffective management behaviors with better ones. Or this judgment may be made about others - parents who want to control their child's destructive behavior, or hospitals wanting to get different behavior from their patients, as in the token-economy experiments discussed earlier. In its most objectionable form, this meaning of behavior control can be stated as the effort to get people to do something that they do not want to do, or else to get them to stop doing what they may very much want to keep on doing.

These two meanings of behavior control - scientific and applied - are not, of course, separate or distinct. The scientific promise that behavior can be controlled in exact and predictable ways has always appealed to those who are responsible for other people. Parents, teachers, judges and police officers, advertisers, politicians - everyone having responsibility or wanting influence - can be attracted to behavior control as a far more sophisticated, exact and efficient way of managing what they have always had to do with threats, persuasion, force or love.

Thus behavior control is not an exact term, but a blend of scientific aspiration and the perpetual search for better management and more effective influence. Control is an emotive word - attracting the manager in us all, but repelling the free spirit in us all.

C. BEHAVIOR MODIFICATION

This book is primarily about behavior modification, not behaviorism or behavior control. Behavior modification is a collective term for all the methods which have been developed in the past several years to use behavioral psychology in the treatment of human difficulties or the enhancement of human possibilities.

Mikulas defines behavior modification as "the application of experimentally established psychological principles to the altering of responses..."[2]

Krasner and Ullmann distinguish between the larger domain of behavior influence and the more specific term, behavior modification. "We have found it convenient to use the term behavior influence as the generic term to include various investigations of the ways in which human behavior is modified, changed, or influenced."[3] Behavior influence, according to these authors, include such procedures as drugs, education, psychotherapy, and advice. "On the other hand, the term behavior modification refers to a very specific type of behavior influence... Studies in behavior modification are studies of learning, with a particular intent - the clinical goal of treatment."[4] In another place, Krasner asserts that behavior modification and behavior therapy mean essentially the same things: "Behavior modification involves the application of principles derived from the psychological laboratory to the changing of undesirable behaviors. It involves a decision on the part of someone who evaluates the social desirability of particular behavior in a given context...

"The term behavior therapy will be used as synonomous with behavior modification procedures designed to alter directly human behavior labeled as deviant."[5]

While it may be desirable to distinguish behavior modification from behavior influence as a more generic process, and while it makes some sense to include the behavior therapies with behavior modification, as do Mikulas and Ullmann and Krasner, other authorities see some difficulties with this procedure. Craighead notes one difficulty with the above definition of behavior modification when he says "...since in a very literal sense any procedure that results in a behavior change may be labeled behavior modification, it is apparent why [definition] is a difficult issue."[6]

Agras is also concerned about the problem of defining behavior modification. He suggests that one way "...is to list the therapeutic procedures which purport to be derived from experiments in learning."[7] But after completing his list, Agras reflects upon the adequacy of that procedure, and suggests "...an alternative is to use the techniques of the behavioral sciences to tease out the principles underlying therapeutic behavior change. ....unfortunately, the behavioral sciences are not advanced enough to allow a comprehensive compilation of the varieties that cause behavior change. For the time being, then, it is necessary to blend these two approaches, moving from therapeutic techniques to experiments analyzing the effective ingredients of such techniques, and from variables which affect behavior to new therapies."[8]

Craighead also proposes a blended definition, after lamenting the vagueness of calling behavior modification whatever is done to change behavior. "An alternative approach is to define behavior modification by its concern with methodology and the functional behavioral relations."[9] Craighead further suggests that such a definition would require that two criteria be met: "1) use of clinical procedures whose descriptions and rationale often rely on experimental findings of psychological research. 2) Experimental and functionally analytic approaches to clinical data, relying on objective and measureable outcomes."[10]

Agras and Craighead obviously do not want to define behavior modification in such a way that it becomes separated from its foundations in the experimental laboratory. While recognizing that many current behavior modification programs are not always that clearly related to specific laboratory findings or learning studies, they want to insist that the connection to research must be a matter of continuing concern for practitioners.

W. Scott Wood suggested the following distinctions: "In the past behavior modifiers were essentially of two groups: applied researchers investigating human behavior with the methods and logic of the basic operant conditioning laboratory (the applied behavior analysts); and clinical psychologists utilizing learning theory in their treatment of clients (behavior therapists)."[11]

Margaret E. Lloyd suggests that the work being done in each of these two areas, behavior modification and behavior therapy, could be spread along a continuum. Such a continuum might begin with basic laboratory research at one end, applied research somewhere in the middle, and therapeutic treatment at the other end.

"Behavior modification spreads across its entire continuum. ...Behavior therapy, however, does not spread entirely across its continuum. There clearly is treatment in behavior therapy. Behavior therapy also occupies the applied research area of its continuum. ...there is very little activity in behavior therapy at the basic research pole of the continuum. Behavior therapy... has already become separated from basic research.... The behavior therapist alters a client's internal responses so that externally he responds differently to an unchanged environment. In this sense, behavior therapy is not that different from more traditional psychotherapies. The behavior modifier, on the other hand, alters the relationship between a client's responses and his environment by changing the environment."[12]

In trying to define behavior modification, we have moved from a single, clear, but very general definition (Mikulas) into complex statements about the relationship of research to practice. Can we come back out with some kind of definition which will be clear enough to be useful but not overly simple?

The difficulty seems to be focused in the connection between research and practice. Researchers rightly object to programs of education or treatment calling themselves "behavior modification" which are not grounded in fundamental research and which do not pursue research issues raised in practice. Practitioners rightly object to research demands which would divert energy and resources from their primary task of helping people.

And this is far more than a professional quarrel between pure and applied sciences. The public interest and the future of behavior modification are at stake. With the spread of behavioral ideas and language in the culture generally, any kind of physical punishment or reward can be called "behavior modification." We do not need the modern science of psychology to tell us that rewards and punishments are effective. Such a total blurring of important distinctions cannot serve either the public welfare or the interests of improved research and practice.

What we need, therefore, is a definition of behavior modification clearly grounded in the modern science of psychology but not so bound to the laboratory that the legitimacy of research in clinical practice is denied. Let me propose the following as such a definition: <u>Behavior modification refers to any program of</u> <u>education or treatment which can be demonstrably derived from the</u> <u>methods and research findings of behavioral psychology, in which</u> <u>environmental factors are the primary agents of change</u>. This definition is sufficiently "tight" to rule out random rewards and punishments, and self-proclaimed "behavior modification" treatment or educational programs with no scientific foundation. It also rules out procedures which invade the organism - drugs, electrode implants or psychosurgery. This proposed definition is "loose" enough in the phrase, "can be demonstrably derived from," so that practitioners can be free to practice without the burden of some second-class status beneath the pure researcher. But the definition does insist that whatever is practiced must be capable of research-grounded demonstration, a responsibility shared by the practitioner and researcher.

D. BEHAVIOR THERAPY

In trying to define behavior modification, it became clear that behavior therapy and behavior modification are terms which are often used interchangeably. Margaret Lloyd's effort to distinguish behavior therapy from behavior modification by the lack of basic research in behavior therapy would surely be challenged by behavior therapists such as Dr. Joseph Wolpe, originator of the systematic desensitization form of behavior modification therapy, who claims to be able to show the superiority of his therapy by his own research efforts.[13]

Even though behavior therapy and behavior modification are often used interchangeably, there is a clear preference for the term behavior therapy when something is so clearly and painfully amiss that treatment is sought - people unable to overcome a fear of closed spaces, caught in self-defeating behavior patterns, anxious, preoccupied, unable to break harmful dependencies. If the clinical procedures used are based upon behavioral or learning theories, then we can call such efforts behavior therapies in contrast to similar efforts to modify the behavior of persons or groups where there is no particularly evident pathology but where some modification is judged to be desirable.

Some examples of behavior therapies might be the best way to illustrate their distinguishing characteristics. Earlier I referred to Joseph Wolpe's method of systematic desensitization. Wolpe has been teaching and practicing systematic desensitization for some twenty years. It involves three elements: training in relaxation, the construction of a graded list of situations which cause anxiety; and practice in the inhibition of the anxiety response.

The client is trained in relaxation procedures which enable the client to achieve a state of physical and emotional relaxation by self-initiated control methods. The graded list of anxiety-producing situations is composed in diagnostic interviews, in which the client, with the help of the therapist, specifies the conditions under which differing degrees of anxiety are experienced. These situations are then grouped and ranked according to the degree of anxiety they produce, from the least to the greatest. The desensitization procedure then consists of therapeutic sessions in which these anxiety provoking situations are imagined and observed, beginning with the least frightening ones. When anxiety is felt, the client employs the previously learned relaxation methods. Therapy proceeds step-by-step until the client is able to imagine or actually confront the most frightening situations without disabling anxiety, because of the increasingly skillful application of relaxation methods.

Another group of behavioral therapies consist of those which use respondent conditioning, of the kind employed by Pavlov and Watson.[14] In this kind of behavior therapy, an undesirable behavior to be eliminated is specified - compulsive eating, smoking, drinking or inappropriate sexual responses, for example. Materials are presented to the client, using pictures, films or other media, which ordinarily would trigger the undesirable behavior, but in conjunction with a painful or unpleasant stimulus. These painful or unpleasant stimuli might include nausea producing drugs (*Clockwork Orange*) or mild but painful electrical shocks. These kind of respondent behavior therapy has been used in cases of severe childhood autism, sexual disorders, chemical dependencies and compulsions.

A special kind of behavioral therapy has been developed by Thomas Stampfl, called "implosive therapy."[15] Based on experiments with reducing fear in animals, implosive therapy consists of "flooding" the client with a barrage of images of the most painful and difficult situations in which the client experiences the most intense anxiety. While implosive therapy has been found to work more quickly than Wolpe's desensitization therapy, there are also studies which indicate that the positive effects of implosive therapy may not be as lasting. Another version of implosive therapy, DiCaprio's technique of verbal satiation, consists of the effort to reduce emotions which are elicited by certain words, by presenting the key words over and over again, until the emotion is extinguished.

A number of applied operant conditioning methods have been developed in behavioral therapies. Probably the best known method is that developed by Ayllon and Azrin known as "token economy."[16] Their initial work was in a mental hospital, where the desired behaviors were identified and then rewarded by tokens which could be exchanged for whatever items or privileges the mental patients might value. By carefully observing the circumstances under which these improved behaviors occurred and by constructing a reward system which truly met the needs of the patients rather than the administrators, Ayllon and Azrin were able to achieve marked improvement in the functioning of many of the mental patients who had previously been judged least likely to improve. Token economy methods have been extended into a number of different settings to deal with many different presenting problems, particularly in the treatment of behavioral disorders in children, in the family and in the classroom.

In their summary of current applications of behavior modification in therapy, Craighead, Kazdin and Mahoney list the following areas: the management of severe anxiety, the treatment of depression, psychiatric and mental hospital treatment, medical and nursing practice, experimental communities, prison treatments, sexual deviation, social skills training, alcohol and drug abuse, obesity, quitting smoking, and behavioral and family problems.[17] In all of these treatments there are certain common features: The client or the persons responsible for defining the problem to be solved enter into a contract with the therapist or the therapeutic team in which the undesirable behaviors (including feelings) are identified, environmental situations or events are specified which are likely to produce these undesirable behaviors or feelings, and then this existing pattern is broken up, and at the same time, new patterns are built which will facilitate the elimination of the undesired behaviors and the practice of more desirable behaviors.

E. SUMMARY AND CONCLUSION

In this chapter I have tried to define four key terms and to give enough historical and illustrative material so that the reader will be better informed about behaviorism and behavior modification. I have defined behaviorism as a school of thought in psychology which has emphasized observable behaviors and the lawful relationships which are presumed to exist between environments and behaviors. I have also identified behaviorism as a pervasive set of assumptions and attitudes in the social sciences and in the helping professions, and increasingly in our culture.

I have defined behavior control as a term which suggests the theoretical if not yet achieved practical ability to establish predictable and repeatable control over behavior through understanding the lawful relationships between environmental causes and behavior of organisms.

I have defined behavior modification broadly as programs of research and application in a variety of therapeutic, educational and social settings, in which the principles of conditioned learning are employed to achieve desired objectives.

And I have defined behavior therapies as those specific forms of behavior modification which are currently applied to the more evident or obvious human difficulties.

With these summary definitions before us, I want to remind the reader again that this book does not concern itself with two other kinds of procedures which are sometimes called behavior modification: electrical or surgical operations on the brain or nervous system, and the use of drugs or other agents which affect moods or perceptions. It is not that these are unimportant matters when assessing methods of behavior control. There are two reasons for these omissions. The scope of the present work is sufficiently comprehensive without considering drugs or the nervous system. But more importantly, the risks inherent in the use of electrical, surgical or chemical interventions are more clearly recognized in research procedures, medical practice and the law, than is the case with behavior modification.

Having introduced some of the issues around behavior modification in Chapter I, and having proposed definitions of key terms in this chapter, we are now ready to turn to the remaining questions of this work: The question of the truth of behavior modification - are we as human beings predictably controlled by events in our environment? - which will be explored in the next chapter. In the fourth chapter, we will examine the question of the rights of the individual and the rights of the community in determining when and for whom behavior modification methods may be used. And in the final chapter, we will examine some implications of behavior modification for the life of religious institutions.

NOTES FOR CHAPTER II

[1]The best brief introduction which clearly defines key terms is by William L. Mikulas, *Behavior Modification: An Overview* (Harper & Row, 1972). A widely used standard text by Albert Bandura is *Principles of Behavior Modification* (Holt, Rinehart and Winston, Inc., 1969). A more recent text, *Behavior Modification, Principles, Issues, and Applications*, (Houghton Mifflin Company, 1976) is by Craighead, Kazdin and Mahoney.

[2]Mikulas, *op.cit.*, 9.

[3]Leonard Krasner and Leonard P. Ullman, *Research in Behavior Modification* (Holt, Rinehart and Winston, 1966), 1-2.

[4]*Ibid.*

[5]Leonard Krasner in *Behavior Therapy: Appraisal and Status*, ed. Cyril Franks (McGraw-Hill, 1969), 539.

[6]Craighead, Kazdin and Mahoney, *op.cit.*, 4.

[7]W. Stewart Agras, *Behavior Modification: Principles and Clinical Applications* (Little, Brown and Co., 1972), 6.

[8]*Ibid.*, 7.

[9]Craighead, Kazdin and Mahoney, *op.cit.*, 5.

[10]*Ibid.*, 6.

[11]W. Scott Wood, *Issues in Evaluating Behavior Modification* (Research Press, 1974), xv.

[12]*Ibid.*, 19-20.

[13]J. Wolpe, *The Practice of Behavior Therapy* (Pergamon, 1969).

[14]The Mikulas and Bandura texts cited above contain helpful descriptions of these treatments.

[15]T. G. Stampfl and D. J. Levis, "Essentials of Implosive Therapy: A Learning-Theory-Based Psychodynamic Behavior Therapy," *Journal of Abnormal Psychology*, 1967, Vol. 72, 496-503.

[16]T. Ayllon and N. Azrin, *The Token Economy* (Appleton-Century-Crofts, 1968).

[17]Craighead, Kazdin and Mahoney, *op.cit.*, ix-xiv.

CHAPTER III: IS IT TRUE?

A. INTRODUCTION

Is it true that <u>all</u> human behavior is caused in ways which can be scientifically demonstrated, and thus predicted and controlled? This is the question to be explored in this chapter.

It is important to explore this question, difficult though it may be, because how we answer determines the way we respond to behavior modification. If we believe that all human behavior is caused, we will regard behavioral explanations as more true than other explanations. And we will assume that behavior modification is more likely to work than other methods, because it more nearly reflects the "way things really are."

But if we believe that human behavior is not caused, or at least not all of it is caused, because we believe in free will, initiative, choice, and the like, then we will conclude that behavioral explanations and behavior modification are not fully adequate.

How is one to decide? As I indicated earlier, we can confront this question only by taking up the issue of free-will and determinism, which has taxed philosophers, theologians and scientists throughout human history. The fact that the free-will and determinism issue has never been satisfactorily resolved leads one to suppose that it may not be capable of resolution as traditionally stated, and to wonder whether renewed attention to it is worthwhile.

These difficulties should surely not be minimized. But I do not see any way to avoid treating this question if we are to work toward an assessment of the degree of truth to be found in behavior modification, an assessment which goes beyond whether we like it or dislike it.

So we shall begin, in the first section of this chapter, by examining what behaviorists themselves claim about the truth of their viewpoint, and how they deal with freedom and determinism. Then we shall survey the way in which the behaviorists' truth claims are approached in the philosophy of science. The following section will sketch a Christian theological stance on free will and determinism. And I will conclude the chapter with a summary statement regarding the implications of this inquiry for behavior modification.

29

B. THE BEHAVIORISTS

1. B. F. Skinner

We will begin this survey with B. F. Skinner. Skinner has consistently advocated what he believes is a strictly scientific understanding of human behavior. In *Science and Human Behavior*, Skinner argues that science involves a certain set of attitudes, namely, a rejection of truth simply on the basis of authoritative claims, believing in facts even when they are opposed to wishes, and the willingness to remain at work on a problem without having achieved an answer. He defines science as the search for order, for uniformities, for lawful relations among events in nature. And he is aware that extending the scientific method from nature to the study of human behavior is filled with difficulties, simply because of the immense complexity of human behavior. Some of Skinner's critics, as we shall soon see, have judged his understanding of science to be inadequate, charging that Skinner views science with a kind of dogmatism which characterized the physical sciences in their pre-modern form.

Why does Skinner value the truth claims of "science" over other ways of knowing the truth? "The methods of science have been enormously successful wherever they have been tried. Let us then apply them to human affairs."[1] A practical test of truth is employed wherever scientific methods have been used--problems are solved which make life better, easier, more convenient.

In another place, Skinner adds a second truth claim. Science not only works. In science, there is progress. New knowledge builds upon previous knowledge. It does not contradict or seek to replace it. Skinner observes that other disciplines, such as art, philosophy, poetry, and theology are not progressive in this sense. He rightly observes that some of the greatest accomplishments in these other disciplines occurred long ago.

Since science works and is progressive, Skinner argues that only by applying scientific methods to the study of human behavior can we bring our understanding of human nature up to the same level as our understanding of natural phenomena.

But Skinner introduces a third criterion for truth which becomes the ultimate norm in his thinking, the truth in which all other truths cohere. Survival is this ultimate norm. We should be using proven scientific methods, he argues, in order that we may guarantee the survival of the human enterprise, and particularly our own culture. Why do we need to worry about human or cultural survival? Because, says Skinner, our presently haphazard cultural arrangements, reflecting our reluctance to apply science to human affairs, or even stubborn opposition, is causing a cultural disintegration which may spell the end of our civilization.

These three criteria for truth - success, progress, survival - are abundantly illustrated throughout Skinner's writings. They appear again as central themes in *Beyond Freedom and Dignity,* the book which brought his ideas to greatest public attention. But he does recast his argument by attacking freedom and dignity so vigorously. Skinner argues that the ideas of freedom and dignity were necessary in human evolution to free humankind from the negative effects of aversive control (punishment), but these controls are weak compared to a scientifically based program of positive reinforcement. In other words, as with the evolution of other species, what were adaptive devices have now become maladaptive, like the now extinct dinosaurs which presumably could not adapt to changes in climate. But Skinner does not want to let nature take its course with humanity. He wants our culture, our human history to survive and grow, so in this book he asks us to give up cherished ideas, like freedom and dignity, to accept scientific causality, and to develop a plan for cultural survival.

We have looked at some of the ways in which Skinner speaks about the truth of behavioral psychology. What is he really saying? Skinner believes in science because it works. And Skinner believes that science is true because it can save human civilization in a time of great peril. (This is not unlike theological truth, or saving truth.) It would not be correct to call Skinner a Darwinian, however, in spite of his references to Darwin and to survival, for Skinner clearly does not believe in "letting nature take its course." So while he accepts the Darwinian analysis of the way by which living species adapt or fail to adapt, Skinner clearly wants us to use all of behavioral technology to guarantee that at least our own specie will not only continue but will also flourish.

We must ask, then, is this truly a scientific view, or is Skinner really propounding a philosophical and moral vision, in which applied science is the chief means of attaining positive human goals? Clearly Skinner's laboratory work and research findings constitute scientific work of the highest order. He will no doubt be judged one of the great psychologists of all time. But his forays into political and moral philosophy must be judged by the criteria appropriate to those disciplines, and not accorded the status which he wants them to have, that of settled scientific conclusions.

Before leaving Skinner, we must examine his discussions of the central question of this chapter: Free will and determinism.

To be a scientist, according to Skinner, one must be a determinist. If there are no causal patterns, no regularities, no senses in which we may infer similar consequences from similar causes, then the whole scientific enterprise breaks down. These are common scientific beliefs. But judgments differ on how to give a scientific account for the human experiences which are variously called freedom, free-will, intention, purpose, and choice. Skinner wants it clearly understood that all such apparently uncaused elements of human experience can be explained on the basis of the individual's genetic makeup and history of conditioning. Like Watson, Skinner rejects all "mentalistic" explanations. There is nothing about internal states like thinking or feeling, reported on by the individual, which can be allowed into a science of human behavior. Whatever people mean when they talk about these things, Skinner believes, can finally be scientifically explained.

In *Walden Two*, Skinner suggests that the feeling of freedom may be important and worthwhile, and, indeed, is likely to be increased in a behaviorally planned society. Frazer says, of *Walden Two*, "... this is the freest place on earth. And it is free precisely because we make no use of force or threat of force.... By skillful planning, by a wise choice of techniques we increase the feeling of freedom."[2] A feeling of freedom, of course, is not to be understood as actual freedom. In reflecting on the debate between Frazer and Castle in *Walden Two*, Frazer says,

> "Doesn't he [Castle] know he is merely raising the old question of pre-destination and free-will? All that happens is contained in an original plan, yet at every stage the individual seems to be making choices and determining the outcome. The same is true of *Walden Two*. Our members are practically always doing what they want to do - what they 'choose' to do - but we see to it that they will want to do precisely the same as which is best for themselves and the community. Their behavior is determined, yet they are free".[3]

Skinner is willing for people to feel free, but they should not suppose that freedom is the actual state of affairs. Two decades later, in *Beyond Freedom and Dignity*, Skinner has come to the conclusion that believing in freedom is a dangerous and outworn ideology which must be explicitly rejected. However, in his most recent book, *About Behaviorism*, Skinner says "feeling free is an important hallmark of a kind of control distinguished by the fact that it does not breed counter-control."[4]

Even if the status of the feeling of freedom is unclear in Skinner's writings, the concept of counter-control qualifies the rigor of his determinism. Counter-control consists of the conditioning procedures used by the subject being controlled to resist the controller or modify the controller. According to Skinner, counter-control is that which will prevent behavioral control methods from being put to despotic uses. In *Walden Two*, Frazer says:

> "...it's a limited sort of despotism... and I don't think anyone should worry about it. The despot must wield his power for the good of others. If he takes any step which reduces the sum total of human happiness, his power is reduced by a like amount. What better check against a malevolent despotism could you ask for?"[5]

In discussing his youthful desire to become a controlling perons, Frazer says,

> "...eventually I realized that subjects are always right. They always behaved as they should have behaved. It was I who was wrong. I had made a bad prediction... and what a strange discovery for a would-be tyrant... that the only effective technique of control is unselfish!"[6]

In *Beyond Freedom and Dignity*, Skinner sees counter-control requiring care and planning.

> "...the great problem is to arrange effective counter-control and hence bring some important consequences to bear upon the behavior of the controller. Some classical examples [prisons, mental hospitals] of a lack of balance between control and counter-control arise when control is delegated and counter-control then becomes ineffective."[7]

In this book, Skinner seems less optimistic than in *Walden Two* about counter-control and control being in automatic harmony and he acknowledges that there must be careful planning to see that justice is maintained. Skinner discusses counter-control further in his most recent book, *About Behaviorism*. In discussing ethics and compassion, he identifies groups of persons who are often assumed not to be treated ethically or with compassion - the young, the aged, prisoners, and the retarded. "It is often said that those who have these people in charge lack compassion or sense of ethics, but the conspicuous fact is that they are not subject to strong counter-control."[8]

This very curious notion of counter-control is hard to pin down. It seems an awkward category for grouping all kinds of limits on simple and perfect control - the given nature of the organism (behavior modification could never get a dog to fly or a fish to walk), or the limits to which living things will allow themselves

33

to be controlled because their interests are violated (you could not modify the behavior of Ayllon and Azrin's mental patients for rewards they did not already value), or something about the requirements of justice and fair play. After struggling to fathom all that Skinner means by counter-control, I wonder why he does not simply talk about resistance, purpose, and justice.

Skinner's notion of counter-control also suggests that he does not really believe in a completely deterministic view at all, but in many ways is a moral philosopher, trying to find ways to use behavioral technology to perserve and enhance a society which is judged to be good because it is successful and progressive. There is simply no way logically for him to maintain a fully deterministic position and at the same time talk about control and counter-control in the ways in which he does. He hopes for a society in which the need for counter-control would no longer exist. There would then be a natural harmony of interests and purposes. In his Utopian vision, then, science becomes the foretaste in the midst of our imperfect society of what is to come, what is to be more fully realized in the perfect society of natural harmony. There, determinism and natural harmony will be one and the same. Until that time, however, in the real world of today, counter-control must be recognized as a positive force for justice, restraining the unchecked power of the controller who might use behavior modification for inhumane purposes.

2. *Other Behaviorists*

We turn now from B. F. Skinner to the writings of other behaviorists. They agree with Skinner that to be truly scientific, one must believe that events do not happen randomly but reflect the lawful operation of causes. But these other behaviorists differ quite widely regarding the degree to which we can ever hope to have a predictable science of human behavior, and in the ways which they find to account for free will. Leonard Krasner asks to what extent can behavior be controlled? "Obviously, at this point, the most reasonable answer is that, given certain types of situations, certain specific behaviors can probably be strongly influenced..." Krasner goes on to say:

"The arguments for the controllability of behavior come from at least three major sources. First it derives from the view of psychology as the science of behavior....Second, there are a growing number of investigations which can be best characterized within the generic term, 'psychology of behavior influence.' ...Third, there are the real life situations in which our behavior is influenced daily by our interactions with others, by education, by newspapers, by parents, by peers, in effect, by the totality of stimulae to which we are continually being exposed."[9]

Krasner does not reject inner states of thinking or feeling, but he does say that even if human behavior is determined by internal events, these can be manipulated by the outside stimuli so that it is these environmental causes which truly determine our behavior. But he says that it is better for people to believe and behave as if they are free to make decisions. Krasner proposes this as a behavioral definition, "...to the extent that a man can believe in terms of having alternative behaviors available, to that extent they are free."[10] Krasner is not so hopeful as Skinner about a behaviorally controlled society. He fears that the control of behavior will be established in such a way that our freedom, "...however defined, will be gone; and, as the crowning blow, we will not be aware of it and we will think of ourselves as free to exist, to be, to become, to grow, and to self-actualize."[11] In a more recent essay, Krasner answers the free-will-determinism question in this way:

> "To state the problem in the simple terms, is man a
> robot or a pilot? The common sense view, based on
> observing human beings, would be that man is both.
> ...Thus man can and should behave as if he were the
> pilot. He is still free to the extent that there is
> no systematic manipulation of his behavior and to
> the extent that he acts as if he were free."[12]

Krasner suggests that there is real freedom if the feeling of freedom is strengthened. Skinner would not agree with that.

Craighead, Kazdin and Mahoney begin their discussion of free-will and determinism by asserting: "In the last few decades psychological research has amply demonstrated that the assumption of determinism is both justified and essential in dealing with human behavior."[13] But these authors go on to distinguish between determinism and predeterminism, which is a fatalistic chain of cause and effect. They argue that events are determined and therefore predictable, at least in principle, but they acknowledge that we cannot now predict with accuracy. However this failure to predict is because of our ignorance rather than any realm of experience outside the domain of causality.

This strict doctrine of determinism becomes modified, however, when these authors discuss responsibility: "...we are responsible in the sense that we usually have at least two alternative response options to choose from and frequently we know what the consequences of those various responses are."[14] If this knowledge of consequences were removed, a significant portion of the controlling environment would be eliminated. Thus human freedom and responsibility become, for these authors, important variables in the prediction and control of behavior."[15] Freedom and responsibility become part of "...the influence process between environment and behavior."[16]

The authors argue that this relationship is not one-way, but that behaviors exert strong controls over environments, as well as environments influencing behaviors. Craighead, Kazdin and Mahoney then ask which comes first - environment or behavior, and they say that this question simply cannot be answered. But they do argue that the individual can take an active role in self-determination. "That is, one can arrange one's environment to produce or eliminate specified behaviors. Does this re-introduce the concept of free-will? No, the act of taking an active role in engineering one's personal environment is determined by previous environmental influences (which may, in turn, have been determined by previous behaviors). However, the interdependence of behavior and environment points to the fact that we are not passive recipients of environmental influence; our performance is a critical determinant of that environment."[17] The authors take up Skinner's idea of counter-control, and agree with Skinner that the implication of determinism is not passivity, but an active use of behavioral technology to enhance one's social and personal life. And so, they conclude, we do have such a thing as "behavioral freedom." "To the extent that we have a wide range of behaviors to draw upon, we are free to react with diversity to environmental influences. This behavioral freedom plays a significant role in personal adjustment and growth."[18] It would seem that such behavioral freedom is no different from freedom as ordinarily conceived, with real choice. So it would appear that these writers, in spite of their efforts to maintain the necessity of determinism from a scientific outlook, are really not determinists at all. There is a real freedom, in the sense that several options are usually available in each moment of choice, so that organisms capable of conscious reflection can weigh the probable outcomes and choose accordingly.

Kanfer and Keroly have taken the idea of a modified determinism one step further. They have developed a scheme for understanding internal as well as external controlling processes. They use the term alpha controls for external, environmental controls, of the type which Skinner and other strict behaviorists ordinarily mean when they talk about any kind of control. Kanfer and Keroly then speak of beta controls as those which would ordinarily be thought of as mentalistic, intra-psychic or "within the skin." These are notions which rigorous behaviorists want to keep out of the science of psychology. Kanfer and Keroly describe their scheme as follows: "...the difficulty in accounting for all human behavior in terms of immediately apparent alpha variables does not force us to go to 'cognitive' theory which postulates different mechanisms for private than for overt behaviors. Instead, the basic behavioral analysis (Skinner, 1953) can be extended to cover both public and private acts."[19] They suggest that "in beta control situations, the individual is hypothesized to make a contract, i.e., to specify performance criteria."[20] They describe the outcome as follows:

"When an individual makes a contract covertly or
with another person (his therapist), the ad hoc
standard of performance promise emerges as a statement of intention... The intention statement may be
one of the critical components of a beta control
sequence, or it may be a terminal link in an alpha
control chain leading to a courageous-appearing
declaration or social approval."[21]

These authors have tried to find a way to talk about decision-making and intending which places these apparently free dynamics with the domain of causality. It is doubtful that Kanfer and Keroly have really rescued the inner life and human agency while remaining determinists. But their effort does demonstrate the concern among behaviorists to maintain scientific determinism along with those uniquely human qualities such as freedom, free-will, intention, purpose, and choice.

We have surveyed what B. F. Skinner and other behaviorists have to say about the scientific character of behavioristic psychology. We have seen that all of them, in one way or another, have defended determinism (broadly understood) as a necessary rule of scientific inquiry. But we have also noted the logical problems which are produced when the principle of determinism is carried into the very core of human self-awareness. There the determinist is confronted with experiences which are difficult to analyze, predict and control - experiences of freedom, purpose and choice. How can these be scientifically explained? One answer is to say that the science of psychology is so new that it cannot yet say. Another approach to this problem by some behaviorists is to find ways of speaking about human experiences like freedom and purpose which affirm some value or use (for Skinner it is low, for certain others like Krasner it is a high value), and then to devise ways of incorporating this modified language of freedom and intention within a behaviorally determined scheme. But these efforts at reassurance have not been particularly successful. Libertarians still fear the possibilities of abuse inherent in behavior control. And the behaviorists themselves have not been able to agree about these matters. That is not a judgment against them. Philosophers, theologians and politicians have not found ways to agree on important matters either. But it does suggest that the current state of psychology as a science and the human subject matter are such that our knowledge is less than exact.

C. PHILOSOPHY AND THE PHILOSOPHY OF SCIENCE

We turn now from Skinner and other behaviorists to the free-will and determinism question as explored in modern philosophy, especially the philosophy of science. While philosophers and theologians have debated free-will through the centuries, the rise of modern science and its application to human research in psychology have focused the issue in particular ways, as philosophers have tried to think through the implications of behavioral determinism.

We will be examining two essays in some detail, because they are penetrating discussions of free-will and determinism in connection with modern science - William James' address on "The Dilemma of Determinism," and Herbert Feigl's essay on "The Mental and the Physical." We will also briefly survey other contemporary discussions in the philosophy of science. But before taking up James and Feigl, it would be helpful to sketch the issues and the options.

A recent book by Edward D'Angelo, *The Problem of Freedom and Determinism,*[22] outlines the options. D'Angelo states that there are four possible viewpoints: (1) libertarianism, which argues that determinism is false and freedom is true; (2) soft determinism, which argues that both determinism and freedom are true in senses which must be carefully specified; (3) hard determinism, which argues that determinism is true and freedom is false; and (4) a logically possible viewpoint which would hold that both determinism and freedom are false, a case which D'Angelo finds that no one has ever argued. D'Angelo provides useful definitions of key terms. Determinism is the belief that every event in the universe is predictable. If we could ever know all of the antecedent conditions of any event, we could predict the event with precision. Most determinists agree, however, that our knowledge is likely always to be quite limited so that we can never attain the accuracy of prediction which this viewpoint affirms as a logical possibility. The determinist argues that while determinism cannot be conclusively proved, determinism is a basic presupposition of all intelligent inquiry. If we did not believe in determinism in some sense, we would never get very far in our efforts to discover the orderly patterns in experience, since chance would prevail. D'Angelo cautions us to remember the difference between determinism and fatalism, and between causality and compulsion. Fatalism reasons that since everything is determined, the only possible human attitude and response is that of passivity.

Soft determinists, in D'Angelo's view, affirm freedom by contrasting it with compulsion, but not with causality. The soft determinist also argues that an individual can be held morally responsible if that person's behavior can be altered in the future by means of reward or punishment. So persons have real choices but always set within a larger framework of cause and effect. A hard determinist, on the other hand, concludes that human beings can never be held responsible for their actions.

Applying this distinction between soft and hard determinists to Skinner and the other behaviorists discussed above, it would seem that everyone, including Skinner, finds some way to affirm responsibility, so they must be soft determinists.

1. *William James*

We turn now to the essay by William James, "The Dilemma of Determinism," written in 1884. James was more than a great psychologist. He was a man of letters and philosophy as well. He was an important representative of philosophical pragmatism. Pragmatism holds that the truth of a philosophical proposition is finely to be determined by its practical effects, not by its correspondence to an underlying structure of reality, an assumption which is central in western philosophy, from Plato to Kant.

As we would expect, William James deals with the question of free-will and determinism by asking the question of the effects of each doctrine. He argues that the problem of free-will versus determinism as ordinarily stated cannot be solved, but that one can discover what difference it makes if one believes in a world of freedom or in a world that is determined.

He begins by emphasizing the importance of the initial starting point, there are:

"...different faiths or postulates - postulates of
rationality. To this man the world seems more
rational with possibilities in it, - to that man
more rational with possibilities excluded; and
talk as we will about having to yield to evidence,
what makes us monists or pluralists, determinists or
indeterminists, is at bottom always some sentiment
like this."[23]

In a very sensitive and probing analysis of the emotional or spiritual character of determinism, James says:

"Determinism, in denying that anything else can be
in its stead, virtually defines the universe as a
place in which what ought to be is impossible, -
in other words, as an organism whose constitution
is afflicted with an incurable taint, an irremediable
flaw."[24]

39

James goes on to argue that this "deterministic pessimism" can become optimism only at the price of extinguishing our judgments of regret. We all have experiences of regret, the evil, pain or suffering which come upon us, the evil we allow or which we actively cause. James argues that the only way to retain any optimism and be a determinist is to become a "subjectivist." The essence of the subjectivist position is the affirmation that we can know but not do the good, that what happens in the universe is subsidiary to what we think or feel about it. "In theology, subjectivism develops as its 'left wing' antinomianism. In literature its left wing is romanticism. And in practical life it is either a nerveless sentimentality or a sensualism without bounds."[25] James finds this kind of subjectivism to be morally and philosophically unacceptable.

He argues, in place of subjectivism, for a philosophy of objectivism.

> "...what is the essence of this philosophy of objective conduct, so old fashion and finite, but so chaste and strong, compared with its romantic rival? It is the recognition of limits, foreign and opaque to our understanding. It is the willingness after bringing about some external good, to feel at peace; for our responsibility ends with the performance of that duty, and the burden of the rest we may lay on higher powers."[26]

James concludes that the only way to maintain such an objective philosophy of moral conduct and its consequences is to affirm the indeterministic way.

> "I cannot understand the willingness to act, no matter how we feel, without the belief that acts are really good and bad... the indeterminism I defend, the free-will theory of popular sense based on the judgment of regret, represents the world as vulnerable, and liable to be injured by certain of its parts if they act wrong... it gives us a pluralistic, restless universe, in which no single point of view can ever take in the whole scene; and to a mind possessed by the love of unity at any cost, it will no doubt, remain forever unacceptable."[27]

There are other reasons, James suggests, why the mind wants the certainty of determinism. Indeterminism... "offends only the naive absolutism of my intellect, - an absolutism which, after all, perhaps, deserves to be subdued and kept in check."[28]

James concludes his essay by relating free-will to a belief in Providence:

"the belief in free-will is not in the least incompatible with the belief in Providence, provided you
do not restrict the Providence to fulminating nothing
but <u>fatal</u> decrees. If you allow him to provide
possibilities as well as actualities in the universe,
and to carry on his own thinking in these two
categories just as we in ours, chances may be there,
uncontrolled even by him, and the course of the universe
be really ambiguous; and yet the end of all things may
be just what he intended from all eternity."[29]

These thoughts remarkably prefigure ideas about divine indeterminism
which are more fully developed in the process philosophy of Alfred
North Whitehead and Charles Hartshorne.

To summarize James' essay, it is clear that while the problem
of free-will and determinism may be logically insoluble, the problem
is still there, and it does matter how we decide. For James, the
deterministic position inevitably leads to pessimism or subjectivism, both having disastrous personal and moral consequences. Determinism is therefore to be rejected. Indeterminism, the belief in
real possibilities, as he preferred to put it, is to be affirmed
because of the moral and practical consequences of holding this view.

2. Herbert Feigl

We turn from the beguiling simplicity of William James to the
far more complex and involved essay on the "The Mental and The
Physical" by professor Herbert Feigl. Feigl belonged to the Vienna
School of Logical Positivism in the late 20's and 30's of this
century, and then came to United States, completing a distinguished
career as Professor of Philosophy at the University of Minnesota,
and as Director of the Center for the Philosophy of Science there.
His essay on "The Mental and the Physical" represented many years
of work on this critical problem of modern philosophy. The problem
of the relationship of the mental to the physical is central to the
question of free-will and determinism. In modern philosophy, the
question of the character of the human mind, and particularly its
relationship to the human body, understood as a very complex and
elaborate machine which nevertheless obeys all of the laws of
science, is a characteristically modern way of dealing with the
subject of free-will and determinism. In other words, if the
relationship between mind and body can be stated, then an answer
to the question of free-will can be given.

Feigl begins with different assumptions from those employed
by William James. Feigl assumes that the goal of finding scientific
concepts to unite the mental and physical dimensions of experience

41

is an appropriate goal, though beset with great difficulty. It is not, in other words, a logically or linguistically insoluble problem. Early in the essay Feigl states the problem in this way: "... the question arises inevitably: how are the raw feels related to the behavioral (or neuro-physiological) states? ... no matter how sophisticated we may be in logical analysis or epistemology, the old perplexities center precisely around this point and they will not down."[30] By "raw feels", Feigl means the way human beings <u>feel</u> about experience as it occurs. He uses this novel term in order to avoid the philosophical implications of more commonly used terms for the "internal" dimensions of experience.

To solve the problem of the relationship of the mental to the physical, Feigl requires that six conditions be met:

First, there must be a thorough analysis and critque of the terms "mental" and "physical".

Secondly, this analysis must do justice to the unity of mind and body which is so widely held today among all of the scientific disciplines engaged in the analysis of human experience.

Thirdly, there must be an analysis of the efficacy of mental states in the behavior of the organism including that which is ordinarily meant by "free-will" or "free-choice."

In the fourth place, there must be a recognition of the experience-based character of statements regarding the correlation of psychological states to neuro-physiological states - that is, how to relate what is reported or stated psychologically to what can be observed in the human organism by means of devices which measure physiological functioning. (Feigl is arguing here that statements regarding the correlation of the two domains must be regarded as empirical statements, that is, capable of validation).

In the fifth place, meaningfulness must be based on intersubjective confirmability. ("Intersubjective confirmability" means that a meaningful statement is one which can be confirmed by a number of observers engaging in the same processes of observation, analysis, and communication among themselves.) Feigl also argues that "immediate experience" can be employed as a basis for confirmation. That is, we cannot rule out what a subject reports as immediate experience simply because it may initially seem incapable of confirmation.

Sixth and finally, Feigl argues that there must be careful analysis of the characteristics in the relationships of the attributes of the mental and physical, in order to arrive at a solution to the problem.

After establishing these formal requirements for an adequate solution to the problem of the relationship of the mental to the physical, Feigl proceeds to construct an argument which meets these criteria. One important conclusion he reaches is that there must be two understandings of the meaning of physical. First, there is the physical domain in the sense in which descriptions are logically connected with the phenomena. The discipline of physics illustrates this first understanding. But there is an important second meaning of the term, physical, and that refers to theoretical statements which are sufficient for explaining the phenomena. He then asks whether the concepts of psychology, particularly those derived from introspection, are physically definable in both senses; not, he answers, with the first understanding of physical, without philosophical analysis, but with the second understanding of the physical, the questions of introspective psychology are an appropriate subject for scientific study, though the conclusions are as yet undecided.

This important distinction leads him to argue for what he calls "neutral monism." In this view, both mentalistic concepts and physical concepts are logically constructed "out of the more basic concepts designating neutral data."[31] He returns to the question of what his analysis does for the "raw feels" which began his inquiry. He says:

> "The basic point is simply that each of us knows his own states of immediate experience by acquaintance, and that by analogical reasoning we can infer similar, though never directly inspectable, states of experience. Direct inspection of the mental states of others is now generally considered a logical impossibility."[32]

That is not to say that we cannot have genuine knowledge of the mental states of other human beings. But it is symbolic knowledge, and does not have the kind of correspondence between reality and interpretation which is supposed to be obtainable by means of naturalistic science. However Feigl prefers to emphasize the unitary character of knowledge.

> "I wish to assert... genuine knowledge is always symbolic, be it acknowledged by acquaintance as formulated in direct introspective report sentences, or be it knowledge by description as, e.g., in the hypotheses of modern nuclear physics."[33]

This affirmation allows Feigl to approve such general concepts as the self or ego.

43

"... whichever of these aspects are in some sense phenomenally 'given' - and I suggest a good many may well be so given - these aspects very likely 'correspond' to (or according to my view, are identical with) certain relatively stable patterns of cerebral structures and functions."34

To summarize Feigl's subtle and complex line of reasoning, it appears that he has addressed the problem of free-will and determinism in two ways: He has tried, first of all, to modify or even loosen the logic and rules of science so that mental phenomena of the kind which Skinner wants to rule out are in fact capable of being subjected to rigorously scientific analysis which is, in no fundamental way, different from the scientific analysis of non-human phenomena. But Feigl clearly does not want to open up scientific reason and principles so far that one resolves the mind - body problem by doing away with science as a law-seeking discipline.

Secondly, Feigl argues that we must hold to a monistic view, a single set of assumptions and rules for scientific investigation and inquiry. We do not need one set of rules for physical phenomena and a different set of postulates and rules for investigating human or mental phenomena. We cannot yet predict what the findings will be regarding the relationship between the psychological domain and the neuro-physiological domain. But Feigl clearly believes that correspondences can and will be discovered which will demonstrate the fruitfulness of a monistic approach.

In comparing Feigl's conclusions with William James', we can see that Feigl would not accept James' pragmatic test of the truth of free-will or determinism, and would argue that James' depiction of determinism is not adequate to account for the kind of unifying science which Feigl advocates.

We have examined these essays by James and Feigl in some detail because they present two important contemporary viewpoints in the philosophy of science on the question of free-will and determinism. James' pragmatism appeals to our common sense, when he says we should believe in freedom because things will go better for us if we do. And since we cannot ever logically settle the free-will-determinism question, let's believe in and act on the better option. Feigl's belief in a unitary science embracing mental and physical phenomena appeals to our commitment to science and our desire to integrate our whole world of experience.

3. *Other Philosophers of Science*

In the concluding part of this section, we will more briefly examine viewpoints on free-will and determinism by other philosophers of science. We will look at three kinds of viewpoints: Those which affirm freedom and reject determinism, those which affirm determinism but reject freedom, and a third group which might be called "middle-of-the-road" positions, (D'Angelo's "soft determinists"), where some kind of reconciliation is achieved by transforming the language of the problem or the argument.

a. Affirmations of Freedom

Sigmund Koch is a noted psychologist and philosopher of psychology who was educated in the behavioral school and identified himself with it for much of his career, but who has rejected the deterministic character of behavioral philosophy. In a symposium on Behaviorism and Phenomenology at Rice University, Koch argues that:

> "... behaviorism has been given a hearing for fifty
> years. I think this generous. I shall urge that it
> is essentially a role - playing position which has
> outlived whatever usefulness its role might once
> have had. If you expect me to support this statement
> via a final and crushing refutation of behaviorist
> epistemology, you will be disappointed. I suspect
> that there is a class of positions that are wrong
> but not refutable and that behaviorism may be in such
> a class. ... if behaviorism is advanced as a meta-
> physical thesis, I do not see what, in final analysis,
> can be done for a truly obstinate disbeliever in mind
> or experience, even by way of therapy. If it is
> advanced as a methodological thesis, I think it can
> be shown that (a) the conception of science which it
> presupposes (especially of concept definition and
> application and of verification) does not accord with
> practice even in those sciences which the position most
> wishes to emulate, and (b) that its methodological
> proposals have had extremely restricted consequences for
> empirical problem selection and a trivializing effect
> upon the character of what are accepted as 'solutions'
> by a large segment of the psychological community."[35]

Koch argues against determinism then, because if it is held as an article of faith, devout believers cannot be dissuaded. But if determinism is used as a set of methods, the results are narrow and trivial. Koch's broadside may be on target for Skinner. But it seems unfair to Feigl's more penetrating defense of a unitary science.

Another tack is taken by G. E. Auscombe in his inaugural lecture at Cambridge. Rather than analyzing the deficiencies of behavioral determinism, Auscombe argues for physical indeterminism. "It has taken the inventions of indeterministic physics to shake the rather common dogmatic conviction that determinism is a presupposition or perhaps even a conclusion of scientific knowledge."[36]

William H. Davis, in his book, *The Free-Will Question*, argues that determinism is simply inconsistent when applied to human beings, since predictions can be taken into account and used to make decisions which may or may not confirm the original prediction. William Ernest Hocking had made the same point in 1928 in his book, *The Self: Its Body and Freedom*, saying:

"... any program which, like that of the behavioristic psychology, aims through the scientific control of human nature to 'predict and control' our behavior ... can only succeed as long as it is kept a profound secret. ... books on applied psychology, on being published, begin the process of defeating their own aim."[37]

In making the case for free-will, Davis argues that while we may legitimately speak of causal tendencies in the physical world and in human behavior, human beings have it in their power to build up new habits or to tear down existing habits, thus altering causal tendencies. He advocates a radical affirmation of free-will. "The doctrine of free-will has radical consequences; it takes away all of our excuses, and leaves us facing ourselves and recognizing that the man we see is of our own creation."[38] Later he argues:

"... it is plain that so far as present psychology goes we are powerless to inaugurate any substantial change in a man against his will, unless perhaps we brain wash him, which is in effect to destroy his mind."[39]

Davis concludes with the assertion that "free-will depends upon reason, and reason depends upon free-will. Without a highly developed reason, the mind cannot break away from its enslavement to the body."[40]

In his book on *The Freedom of the Will*, Austin Farrer examines the physical explanation of thinking as the way of judging between free-will and determinism. He finds behavioral determinism deficient in two respects: (1) we are so limited in being able to describe thinking, decision-making or the directing of voluntary movement by physiological analysis, that we ought not to be required to accept determinism over free-will.

> (2) "They [psychologists] may be doctrinaire determinists, to a man. We are not concerned with their opinions, but with their achievements. Do either require them to presuppose determinism, or oblige them to conclude it? When we speak of their achievements or of what they do, we adopt the tone of strict empiricalism. Can they control, can they predict?"[41]

Farrer believes that the psychologists can neither control nor predict, so their arguments for determinism have no foundation.

We have just examined a sampling of viewpoints which reject determinism and affirm free-will. They all have much in common with the viewpoint of William James. Since we cannot demonstrate the fact of determinism or the necessity of assuming it, and since we can point to so many evidences that there is genuine choice among several options, a science of human behavior which denies free-will must be rejected because it leaves out an important part of human experience.

b. Affirmations of Determinism

Now we turn to representative statements from those in the philosophy of science who affirm determinism, or who support behavioral psychology as a deterministic science.

R. B. Joynson in *Psychology and Common Sense* develops an argument which has aims in common with Feigl and Skinner.

> "... from the standpoint of objective science, the explanation of behavior must be sought in the brain. ... clearly this view marks the end of the behaviorist belief that psychology seeks laws of behavior independently of physiology, for now it is neurology which is to provide the basic principles."[42]

Phillip H. Scribner[43] argues that Skinnerian behaviorism has failed because it has left out all mentalistic or intentional concepts. He believes that omission seriously limits behaviorism as a comprehensive explanation of human behavior. He argues that events in the mind can, in principle, be behaviorally observed since they depend upon physical processes for their origination and transmission. The solution for behavioral psychology, therefore, is not

47

to draw such a narrow boundary around acceptable concepts, but to extend its purview to include "inner" dimensions of experience which Skinner has declared out of bounds.

R. L. Franklin in *Free-will and Determinism* also argues:

"... that an adequate neuro-physiology will eventually erode the assumption usually made by determinists and libertarians alike; namely of the assumption that we could in principle specify with unlimited precision the state of affairs which would turn out to be, or fail to be, sufficient for its successor."[44]

Franklin further argues that Heisenberg's principle of indeterminism in physics, when applied in psychology, will help to resolve the question of free-will and determinism.

Kendon Smith also advocates determinism. Like Joynson, Scribner, and Franklin, Smith argues that conscious experience must be taken into any scientific psychological analysis. He sums up his case this way:

"I believe it is clear that the present series of essays tends to reinforce such a responsible plea for the readmission of introspective evidence to court. It does so mainly, perhaps, through its arguments in support of physical monism. ... it follows from the latter view that awareness, being part of the material world itself, is in principle entirely public."[45]

Smith's indebtedness to Feigl is evident here. Smith concludes that the so-called humanistic psychology must be rejected on scientific grounds, but Skinnerian behaviorism must also be rejected since it leaves out human consciousness.

These selections from philosophers of science who espouse determinism are disappointing when compared with Skinner's arguments for determinism. While it may simply be that Skinner thinks and writes more clearly, there is more to it than that. These philosophers of science who make a case for determinism (including Feigl) are trying to include inner states of thinking, feeling and choosing within a unitary and deterministic science. Skinner leaves all that out. So the clarity of his argument is purchased at a steep price. We may find the arguments confusing and complex which try to integrate inner human experience into a deterministic and physical explanatory framework. But at least Feigl and these other determinists are struggling to construct concepts and language which are inclusive, not exclusive like Skinner.

c. "Middle-of-the-Road" Viewpoints

We turn now to examples in the philosophy of science where
some kind of effort is made to transform the free-will-determinism
problem into something else, or combine elements in a new synthesis.

Norman Malcolm, in the same Rice University Symposium on
Behaviorism and Phenomenology mentioned earlier, agrees that Skinner
has stated decisively the objections to introspectimist psychology.
But he criticizes behaviorism for leaving out statements of intention.
"The 'Achilles heel' of this doctrine lies in its treatment of
psychological sentences in the first - person present tense."[46]
Malcolm explains that "...the natural temptation to which behaviorist
philosophers have succumbed is to assume that first-person psychological sentences have the same 'content,' or the same verification
as the corresponding third-person sentences."[47] Malcolm argues
that both behaviorism and introspectionism are incorrect in
supposing that these sentences are based on the observation of
events. There is a class of first-person-present statements which
do not require any observation, but which are simply statements of
intention. "... we have no ground at all for believing either intentions or announcements of intention are under the 'control' of
anything." He goes on to say that:

> "...the first-person psychological sentences must be
> correlated with behavior up to a point. But they
> quickly go beyond that point. People tell us things
> about themselves which take us by surprise, things
> which we should not have guessed from our knowledge of
> their circumstances and behavior. A behaviorist
> philosopher will say that if we had known more about
> their history, environment, and behavior, we should
> have been able to infer the same information. I do
> not believe there are any grounds for thinking so.
> The testimony that people give us about their inten-
> tions, plans, hopes, worries, thoughts, and feelings
> is by far the most important source of information we
> have about them. This self-testimony has, one could
> say, an _autonomous_ status. To a great extent we cannot
> check it against anything else, and yet to a great
> extent we credit it. I believe that we have no
> reason to think it is even a theoretical possibility
> that this self-testimony could be supplanted by
> inferences from external and/or internal physical
> variables."[48]

Malcolm summarizes his criticism of behaviorism in this way:

"... behaviorism, fails to perceive that self-testimony
is largely autonomous, not replaceable even in principle
by observations of functional relations between physical
variables. Perhaps the best way to sum up behaviorism
shortcoming as a philosophy of psychology is to say
that it regards man as <u>solely</u> an <u>object</u>."[49]

Charles Taylor[50] represents another kind of middle-of-the-road
position. He transforms the free-will-determinism problem by
setting it within the framework of hermeneutics, which is the discipline of interpretation. Taylor suggests that the two great
systems of modern philosophy - rationalism and empiricism - have
both tried to break out of the hermeneutical circle, by trying to
establish the "real" meaning of the "brute data," so that there
is a perfect correspondence between reality and interpretation.
Taylor says that there can never be such a perfect correspondence,
that reality is always interpreted within what he calls "the
hermeneutical circle," so that it is literally impossible to do
more than approximate the rules of science. A human science would
be sterile, says Taylor, if it tried to be so methodologically pure
that it denied the full reality of experience. Here Taylor echos
Koch.

George Mandler and William Kersen argue that physicalism, the
belief that human bodies are physical systems governed by physical
processes, does not mean that non-physical variables cannot influence, cause or determine physical actions.

"Thus we assert the need for the belief in freedom
even in the absence of any evidence for the doctrine.
Individuals make determined decisions to choose and
once choosing make deterministic (including of
course probablistic) choices. But the likelihood
that such choices contribute to their humanity is
increased by their belief in the doctrine. Thus,
even the most violent opponent of the doctrine
not only does but should believe in the exercise
of his daily choices."[51]

Here Mandler and Kersen repeat the argument of William James.

Howard Hintz has proposed a solution to the free-will and
determinism question based upon the Process of Philosophy of Alfred
North Whitehead. "Once reality is seen as process and nature as
organism, the problem disappears."[52] Hintz offers the following
Whiteheadian propositions concerning the mind - body problem: First,
mind is inseparably associated with and dependent upon the physical
organism. Secondly, we have no real knowledge of sources, causes,

origins, or essential nature of activities called "mental." We know that physical organs like the brain and the glands are involved, but we also know that it is always an involvement of mutual cause and effect. Thirdly, mind and body are equally parts of the natural order. Fourth, all theories of mind or spirit which go beyond the natural are untested, unproved, and thus belong in the class of symbolic or poetic expressions. Fifth and finally, a Whiteheadian approach would clearly state that nature cannot be separated into two realms such as mind and body anyway.

These examples of attempts in the philosophy of science to redefine the problem of free-will and determinism or to restate the basic concepts in ways in which the problem is transformed suggest solutions to the problems posed by Skinner and his critics. But a word of caution is in order. None of us is a stranger to the problem of free-will and determinism. We all have experienced situations of being determined <u>and</u> free. It will not work simply to say that it is a false problem. Our language, concepts and arguments may lead us astray, but no refinements of language or interpretation will solve the problem.

4. *Conclusions from Philosophy and the Philosophy of Science*

In summarizing and evaluating the contributions of philosophy and the philosophy of science to the problem of free-will and determinism, I would propose the following general conclusions: First of all, these philosophical discussions are more penetrating and comprehensive than the writings of B. F. Skinner or other behaviorists. And we should surely not expect psychologists to be philosophers. Their research, teaching and professional practice do not require that they be systematic philosophers. But where Skinner and the other behaviorists discuss free-will and determinism, we look in vain for the depth or clarity of analysis that we found in the philosophy of science.

Secondly, the claim that behaviorism must be a deterministic science is qualified at so many points in so many different ways, that any simple advocacy of determinism like Skinner's cannot be supported. On this point, Skinner stands alone.

Thirdly, a science of human behavior must be formulated in such a way as to take account of those dimensions of human experience which are variously called "mentalistic", "introspectionist," intending, choosing, willing, and deciding. There are different ways proposed for including that experience, to be sure. But it seems agreed, given all of these differences, that we cannot have two fundamentally different sciences of the human - one for mental life, and one for physical or behavioral life.

Fourth, a unitary science of human behavior will be like other scientific disciplines, in formulating highly probable or law-like statements about events. These statements will then be tested through prediction. Within that framework, ways will be found to account for what Malcolm calls intention or choice.

And Fifth, there is such a thing as the human will; it does constitute a set of functions like intending and choosing and deciding; and a unitary science of the human, one which will enable us to predict and control with high degrees of probability, must take that dimension fully into account. The behaviorism of B. F. Skinner cannot do that. But as we have seen, other behaviorists and philosophers have devised ways to affirm intention and choice.

D. CHRISTIAN THEOLOGICAL TRADITION

In trying to decide whether all human behavior is caused and can be predicted, or whether there is free-will or choice, we began by consulting the psychologists and then the philosophers. Even the patient reader may have grown restless by now, with the slow pace of examination and analysis, still yielding no clear and simple answer.

But I must ask for even greater forbearance. As indicated in the first chapter, I write as a Christian theologian. So I must approach any question of truth, including free-will and determinism, within a theological perspective. While it is necessary to examine the truth claims of the psychologists and philosophers, it can never be theologically sufficient to adopt one or another such view on its own terms, whether it be James or Feigl or Skinner. We must always judge which truth claims more nearly approximate those of faith, but even where that approximation is close, the grounds for judgment differ. Faith claims to know truth through knowing God, since all truth coheres in God. Psychology and philosophy claims to know truth by knowing something about how truth is discerned. God is not a necessary postulate for them.

I hope that non-theological readers will not be unduly put off by what may seem a useless or annoying detour. I hope they will at least follow the discussion through to the end, where I do promise a kind of solution to the problem of free-will and determinism, based upon a theological integration of the psychological and philosophical views surveyed.

1. Scriptures

We begin with the scriptures of the Judaic and Christian traditions. As it is with so many questions, one cannot derive from the

Old or New Testament writings a clear or conclusive point of view regarding free-will and determinism. The scriptures are not that systematically philosophical. We can, however, identify some important themes in scripture which suggest a framework within which to examine subsequent Christian writing.

First of all, in both the Old and New Testaments, the depictions of the creation of the human race, the destiny to which the people of Israel are called, their Exodus from Egypt and their national formation in Canaan, the message of the Prophets, the Exile in Babylonia and the postexilic restoration, - all of these materials point to a belief that human beings are indeed free to accept or reject the claim which God offers. Often enough they exercise their freedom by turning away from God. This same theme is reasserted in the Gospels. The message and ministry of Jesus are for the purpose of persuading people that the time of the Kingdom is at hand, and that they ought to repent and believe in this good news. Surely this form of address implies the freedom to accept or reject the gospel. It is only in the letters of Paul that the theme of election or predestination is emphasized to account for human salvation. And Paul emphasizes election as a sign of God's gracious mercy, with no logical conclusions about human action as totally determined.

Along with this persistent emphasis upon human freedom and choosing, the scriptures of the Old and the New Testaments also point to the freedom and power of God, with the clear affirmation that the events of nations and peoples, and, indeed, the events of nature and the cosmos move at God's command. The way in which God's will is exercised through human and natural events is not known or clearly understood, but simply accepted as the ultimate explanation. The Jewish and Christian scriptures do not allow for any rival or intermediary powers at work in human affairs or nature which explain what is really going on.

This theme of God's ordaining or determining will, of God as the ultimate ground and cause of all that is, does find partial qualification in particular texts and traditions which become part of the scriptures, where the powers of evil are used to explain what is happening. Usually this evil power is derived from humanly evil decisions and actions. That is, people have sinned against God, so that destructive consequences are understood as punishment justly meted out. In the apocalyptic literature in both Old and New Testaments, the powers of evil are identified with the figure of Satan. Thus human and natural misfortune are attributed to the powers of evil which have taken over in place of God. Life thus becomes a cosmic battleground between the divine and demonic powers. But even where the scriptures move toward a cosmic dualism of good and evil, they continue to promise that God will triumph over evil, so that a permanent dualism is rejected.

In these scriptures, God's power and the powers of evil do indeed impinge upon human affairs in determining ways. But it is not the kind of logical determinism which Skinner insists is the character of modern science. That kind of logical rigor (or rigidity) is simply not characteristic of the thought-world of the communities which produced the scriptures, and is not found in the kind of literature which constitutes scripture.

It is of course possible to "find" both free-will and determinism in the scriptures. Particular texts and concepts can be taken from the scriptures in order to build a case that either free-will or determinism is the scriptural view. That kind of extrapolation is evident in some of the theological writings we shall be examining shortly. But that method of proof-texting does not faithfully represent the full scope of the scriptural traditions.

While the scriptures affirm human freedom and choice, it is clearly a limited freedom, limited by the fact that God's directing will is the final cause at work in human and natural affairs, and also limited by the consequences of bad human choices. This act of choosing badly, of deciding against God's purposes and claims rather than for them, is understood to result in a progressive loss of human capacities, including the ability to choose and act wisely.

2. Gregory and Augustine

The early Christian theologians struggling with the task of restating the Christian Faith with the images and in the categories of Greek philosophy and culture, continued to affirm the themes of human freedom and God's determining will. Gregory of Nyssa, one of the great Greek Father's of the fourth century, writing in his *Great Catechism* argues for free-will on the basis of humanity's creation in the image of God.

> "Was it not, then, most right that that which is in
> every detail made like the Divine should possess
> in its nature a self-ruling and independent principle,
> such as to enable the participation of good to be
> the reward of its virture?"53

Later in this same work, Gregory argues that one of the implications of free-will in humanity is that God could not forceably impose salvation upon the unwilling.

> "For they [opponents against whom Gregory writes]
> assert that God, if He had been so pleased, might
> have forceably drawn those, who were not inclined
> to yield, to accept the Gospel message. But where

then would have been their free-will? Where their
virtuous merit? Where their need of praise from
their moral directors? It belongs only to inanimate
or irrational creatures to be brought around by the
will of another to his purpose; whereas the reasoning
and intelligent nature, if it lays aside its freedom
of action, loses at the same time the gracious gift of
intellect."[54]

This emphasis on free-will in early Christian writers was in
part addressed to groups in the Christian community which were
adopting Gnostic and Neoplatonic ideas of divine emanations. In
such mythologies, evil is caused by lesser divinities. Gregory,
and his great teacher, Origen, argued that evil is not caused by
inferior deities or by the evil of the material world, but is
produced by freely willed human actions.

By the time of St. Augustine, changing circumstances in the
Christian world and Christian thought had led western theology away
from Gregory's clear insistence on free-will. This shift can be
seen in the writings of Augustine on free-will and determinism. In
his first essay on Free-Will, dated probably in 395 or 396 A.D.,
Augustine is primarily addressing the Manichaeans. He begins with
an exposition which demonstrates that God is both good and just.
Man is held to be superior to the beasts in possessing reason. When
reason rules, a person is wise. Hence, he argues that sin is voluntary, and that man's present state of ignorance and inability is the
just penalty of voluntary sin. Free-will, which is necessary for
the good life, may be used badly by seeking to attain its own private
ends. This turning away from true good to evil is, according to
Augustine, purely voluntary. Its only cause is in the human will.
God is not to be made the agent of human sinning.

Later, this treatise on the free-will was used against him by
the Pelagians (followers of Pelagius, a British Monk who rejected
the doctrine of original sin and advocated the view that every human
being is born with the capacity for good or evil). Augustine saw
in the Pelagian teachings a clear threat to the Christian belief in
a complete dependence upon God's grace for salvation. In these
changed historial circumstances, no longer contending against Gnostic
and Neoplatonic notions of evil present in matter and inferior deities,
it becomes necessary to reexamine the earlier writings on free-will,
and Augustine does so in a catalog of retractions and also in a new
treatise on Grace and Free-will, which was written in A.D. 426 or
A.D. 427.

In the Retractions, Augustine warns the Pelagians not to employ
his earlier treatise wrongly. He says he was not discussing God's

grace in the earlier essay, and the Pelagians should not conclude that human freedom is independent of God's grace.

> "Certainly, will is that by which a man sins or lives righteously, as I argue in these words. But mortals cannot live righteously and piously unless the will itself is liberated by the grace of God from the servitude to sin into which it has fallen and is aided to overcome its vices."[55]

In the Retractions, Augustine classifies free-will among the good things which come from God:

> "Free-will was put among the medium goods, because we can make a bad as well as a good use of it, and yet it is good because we cannot live righteously without it. ....because all good things, as I said, great, medium and small, come from God, it follows that from God also comes the good use of free-will, which is virtue, and which is numbered among the greater goods."[56]

In his later essay on Grace and Free-will, Augustine begins his argument by asserting that God created humankind with free-will so that sinners in no way could excuse themselves from the evil into which their lives have fallen. The doctrine of free-will protects God from blame as a possible originator or creator of evil. He goes on to argue that while free-will is a necessary assumption, it is entirely mistaken to interpret teachings on free-will in any way which leaves no room for the operation of grace. It is finally God's grace which enables the human will to turn again to God.

Having addressed these admonitions against the Pelagians, Augustine asks whether God can convert wills opposed to God. He argues from many texts of scriptures that God is able to do so. Not wanting to be regarded as having abolished an independent will altogether, however, Augustine adds: "...there is, however, always within us a free-will, - but it is not always good; for it is either free from righteousness when it serves sin, - and then it is evil, - or else it is free from sin when it serves righteousness, - and then it is good."[57] For Augustine, then, freedom has become the condition of human beings in grace, whereas an unfree will is a will that is in bondage to sin. This radically altered understanding of freedom comes to characterize the writings of Augustine and other Christian theologians who have emphasized the radical bondage of human sin and the radical dependence upon God's grace which is required in order to be saved, and thus regain freedom.

But again Augustine modifies the strictness and harshness of his formula. He says that the person who wishes to do God's will, but is unable to do so, still possesses a good will, "...but yet a small and weak one."[58] So, he says, in salvation, the human will is not taken away, but changed from a bad will to a good will, and then given further assistance by God's grace.

Toward the end of this essay, Augustine tries to account for the ways in which the divine will interacts with human wills: "...God works in the hearts of men to incline their wills whithersoever He wills, whether to good deeds according to His mercy, or to evil after their own deserts; His own judgment being some times manifest, some times secret, but always righteous."[59] So, for Augustine, human freedom, particularly the freedom to choose the good, is decisively lost in the fall. Human beings are incapable of willing and doing the good. In nature and in the scriptures, there are evidences of the good, so the knowledge of the good is available, and people are therefore without excuse in their failure to will and to do the good. But it is only when God gives grace that this evil will is transformed into a good will, and the fruits of faith and good works can follow. Thus while Augustine affirms the freedom of human will in a formal sense, the will has in fact been rendered powerless for good through sin. The decisive power by which the will can be rescued belongs to God alone.

Western Christian theological thought has been profoundly shaped by this Augustinian formulation. Reformers in every Christian period, but particularly in the Protestant Reformation of the sixteenth and seventeenth century, looked to Augustine (and to Paul) for support in their own reaffirmation of the radical dependence of the Christian believer on God's grace, and an equally radical rejection of any vestige of the human capacity to will and choose the good. The conflict between Calvinists and Arminians in the eighteenth century, and the conflicts between theological liberals and conservatives in contemporary Christendom can be seen as altered but continuing forms of this same debate.

3. *Thomas Aquinas*

This Augustinian emphasis upon the bondage of the human will to sin and the loss of meaningful freedom is not the only major treatment of this theme in Western Christian Theology. In the middle ages, Thomas Aquinas took up this same theme in his discussions of providence and predestination. Employing Aristotle's types of causes, Aquinas begins by defining and distinguishing particular causes and a universal cause, to which all particular causes are subordinated. He says that "...the activity of man's free-will still derives from God as its cause, so that whatever he does by means of it is still under the rule of God's providence."[60] But that does not mean that the human will is predetermined. "Providence imposes a necessity on some things but not all things - contingent beings required contingent causes - necessary beings require necessary causes."[61]

Aquinas then argues that predestination is not the same as natural necessity.

"Predestination achieves its effect most certainly and infallibly ... but it does not impose necessity of such a kind that its effect is realized through necessity. ... it [pre-destination] does not exclude the freedom of the will, but realizes its effects contingently by means of it."[62]

In another place, where Aquinas is discussing the question of whether all events that take place in this world are determined or fortuitous, he says the following:

"...with regard to the divine will, remember that it is not like ours. It transcends the system of particular things, of which it is the cause: God's will suffuses the whole of reality and all its shades of variety. Consequently necessity and indeterminancy enter into things from the divine will itself. The distinction applies to events from the nature of their approximate causes. To effects which he wills to be necessary God provides necessary causes; to effects he wills to be free he provides contingently active causes, that is, causes able to act otherwise. The nature of the approximate causes settles whether an effect should be called necessary or contingent. Yet every effect depends on the divine will as on the first cause which transcends the system.

"This cannot be said of the human will, or indeed of any creative cause, for all causes, except God, are confined in a system of necessity or contingence, whether they be variable or constant in their activity. The divine will cannot fail, but we cannot therefore ascribe necessity to all its effects."[63]

In the Summa Theologica, Aquinas affirms that,

"...man has free choice, otherwise counsels, exertations, precepts, prohibition, rewards, and punishments would all be pointless."

...in explanation note that some things act without judgment, as when a stone falls; others with judgment but more from natural instinct than deliberate adjustment, as when a sheep flees from a wolf. Man, however, can

act from judgment and adaptation in the reason; a free
judgment that leaves intact the power of being able
to decide otherwise. The reason keeps an open mind,
as appears in dialectical proofs and rhetorical
persuasions. Particular lines of conduct are contingent. Concerning any one of them the practical reason
is not committed before hand. A man has free choice to
the extent that he is rational."[64]

In Contra Gentes, Aquinas distinguishes between effects upon the
will from external causes and effects produced by God.

"The will's mastery over its own activity, its inner
power to decide or not, excludes predetermination by
another particular cause and violence from an external
agent, but not the influence of a higher cause which
is the principle alike of its own being and of its
activity. The causality of the first cause flows into
movements of will, and so God in knowing himself knows
these as well."[65]

In another treatise, Aquinas asks:

"Does Divine predestination impose necessity on human
acts? In this matter we must proceed cautiously so
that truth may be strengthed and error avoided. For
it is equally false to say that human acts and events
do not fall under Divine foreknowledge and that foreknowledge and the Divine predetermination load human
acts with necessity, for that would abolish freedom,
the opportunity of giving counsel, the usefulness of
laws, the care for acting aright, and the fairness of
rewards and punishments."[66]

This survey of texts from the writings of Thomas Aquinas shows
that his use of the Aristotelian philosophical framework required him
to affirm real human choice, because of the dominance of reason as
uniquely human. It is of the very essence and character of reason
to be able to weigh alternative ideas, to anticipate consequences,
and to make genuinely free decisions among existing alternatives.
There was no way in which Aquinas could understand the fall and human
sin to have obliterated reason and free-will. While he clearly
affirmed human dependence upon God's grace for salvation, at the
decisive point of the human reception of God's grace, the freedom
of the will is not excluded, but rather salvation is received and
its effects realized by means of the will.

The great Protestant Reformers of the sixteenth century, as indicated earlier, looked to Augustine and to Paul for support in reasserting the radical depravity of the human will, and the radical dependence upon God's grace which was required for salvation. They traced abuses in the church to doctrines and practices which unduly emphasized the human role in attaining salvation. The abuses of indulgences which aroused Martin Luther suggested that human action determined salvation. It also seemed to the Reformers that penance, the veneration of relics and shrines, and popular belief about the effects of masses and prayers for the dead all lent themselves to the same erroneous theological conclusions - that human beings had some domain of free choice or will regarding their own salvation.

Martin Luther's treatise on the *Bondage of the Will,* directed against Erasmus' essay on the freedom of the will, states the classical Reformed view. He argues that free-will must be rejected as a consequence of the biblical doctrine of grace. The heart of the gospel was at stake. Luther was not advocating determinism. He acknowledged that human choices are real. But he insisted upon the belief that human beings had no choice in the drama of salvation. Luther put it this way:

> "If we do not want to drop this term (free-will) altogether - which would really be the safest and most Christian thing to do - we may still in good faith teach people to use it to credit man with 'free-will' in respect, not of what is above him, but of what is below him. That is to say, man should realize that in regard to his money and possessions he has a right to use them, to do or to leave undone, according to his own 'free-will' - though that very 'free-will' is overruled by the free-will of God alone, according to His own pleasure. However, with regard to God, and in all that bears on salvation or damnation, he has no 'free-will,' but is a captive, prisoner, and bond slave, either to the will of God or to the will of Satan.[67]

This distinction is emphasized later in the same treatise. Luther addresses Erasmus: "you are no doubt right in assigning to a man a will of some sort, but to credit him with a will that is free in the things of God is too much."[68]

In his *Institutes of the Christian Religion,* John Calvin attempts a more systematic statement than Luther's. Calvin begins by stating that there are three faculties in the soul, understanding, sense, and appetite or will.[69] Understanding refers to what we would more typically call reason. <u>Sense</u> refers to the emotions. And <u>will</u>

refers to intending and choosing. Calvin argues that understanding
is a superior quality, emotions or sense are inferior human characteristics, and that the will is placed in the middle station between
reason and sense, "...as perfectly at liberty, whether it chooses
to obey reason, or to submit to the violence of sense."[70] Calvin
reviews the history of this doctrine in the Greek and Latin Church
Fathers, affirming the basic principles asserted by Augustine and
observing that Aquinas tended to equate will and reason. Calvin
concludes, from these earlier writers, that "...man is not possessed
of free-will for good works, unless he is assisted by grace, and that
special grace which is bestowed on the elect alone in regeneration."[71]
In specifying the condition of the will in the fallen or sinful state,
Calvin says:

> "...the will, being inseparable from the nature of man,
> is not annihilated; but it is fettered by depraved and
> inordinate desires, so that it cannot aspire after
> anything that is good. ...to condemn it to perpetual
> blindness, so as to leave it no intelligence in any-
> thing, is repugnant, not only to the Divine Word, but
> also to the experience of common sense."[72]

Calvin employs the terms "terrestrial things" and "celestial things"
to identify the domains of human experience in which fallen humankind
continues to have some valid knowledge and some genuine freedom.
"Celestial things are the pure knowledge of God, the method of true
righteousness, and the mysteries of the heavenly kingdom."[73] Under
the category of terrestrial things, Calvin lists civil polity,
domestic economy, all the mechanical arts and liberal sciences. He
discusses these terrestrial disciplines in some detail, and argues
that since all truth comes from God, even that light of truth which
enlightens fallen human minds should be received and appreciated.
"...let us learn from such examples, how many good qualities the
Lord has left to the nature of man, since it has been despoiled of
what is truly good."[74]

Using this distinction between terrestrial and celestial things,
Calvin examines the human will. The will is commonly thought to be
exercised in the freedom of choice. But Calvin cautions,

> "...let us observe, that the power of free choice
> is not to be contemplated in that kind of appetite,
> which proceeds rather from the inclination of the
> nature than from the deliberation of the mind. ...man
> neither rationally choses as the object of his pursuit
> that which is truly good for him, according to the
> excellency of his immortal nature, nor takes the advice
> of reason, nor duly exerts his understanding; but without
> reason, without reflection, follows his natural inclina-
> tion, like the herds of the field. It is therefore no

argument for the liberty of the will, that man is led
by natural instinct to desire that which is good; but
it is necessary that he discern what is good according to right reason; that as soon as he knows it, he
chose it; and as he has chosen it to pursue it."[75]

Thus Calvin rejects any belief that the will is naturally good. And
he also reveals his affinity with the classical and medival view
that human goodness is to be found in reason, whereas evil arises
from the instincts and emotions.

Calvin then argues that:

"...the will ...is so bound by the slavery of
sin, that it cannot excite itself, much less devote
itself to anything good; for such a disposition is
a beginning of a conversion to God, which in the
scriptures is attributed solely to Divine grace."[76]

Just as Augustine did not want such a definition to be taken to mean
the annihilation of the will, so Calvin hastens to add:

"Nevertheless there still remains the faculty of
will, which with the strongest propensity is inclined
to and rushes into sin; for when man subjected himself
to this necessity, he was not deprived of his will, but
of soundness of will ...therefore simply to will belongs
to man; to will what is evil, to corrupt natures; to
will what is good, to grace."[77]

Again, like Augustine, Calvin insists that this loss of a sound will
is not destined, but chosen.

"We must therefore observe this grand point of
distinction, that man, having been corrupted by his
fall, sins voluntarily, not with reluctance or
constraint; with the strongest propensity of disposition, not with violent coercion; with the bias of his
own passions and not with external complusion: yet
such is the depravity of his nature, that he cannot
be excited and biased to anything but what is evil."[78]

Thus the freedom of the will continues to be exercised voluntarily
only in choosing evil. Free-will cannot be employed to choose the
good without the aid of divine grace. To the modern mind, this may
not seem a very substantial or genuine understanding of freedom. But
such a formulation is required by the assumptions and logic with
which Calvin worked.

Calvin next describes what happens to the will when God's grace acts upon it.

"If, therefore, when God converts us to the pursuit
of rectitude, this change is like the transformation
of a stone into flesh, it follows, that whatever
belongs to our own will is removed, and what succeeds
to it is entirely from God. The will, I say, is
removed, not considered as the will; because, in the
conversion of man, the properties of our original nature
remain entire. I assert also, that it is created anew,
not that the will begins to exist, but that it is
then converted from an evil into a good one. This I
affirm to be done entirely by God. ..."[79]

Thus Calvin specifically rejects any idea of the necessary cooperation of the will in salvation (Gregory of Nyssa, for example): '...He [God] moves the will, not according to the system maintained and believed for many ages, in such a manner that it would afterwards seem at our option either to obey the impulse or to resist it, but by an efficacious influence."[80]

To summarize Calvin's doctrine of free-will, we observe that the will is placed, somewhat like the ego in contemporary psychology, between the higher powers of reason and the lower powers of sense. In the fall into sin, human reason is darkened but not lost. So Calvin can affirm the works of philosophers, scientists, artists, political philosophers and others as possessing genuine insight into truth, even if it is not the truly important knowledge which is required for salvation. But in the fall into sin, the will becomes an evil will, still free in a limited fashion, but free only in the sense of pursuing its own sinful and depraved ways. Taking these together - the darkening of reason and the depravity of the will - we arrive at a kind of fallen human existence in which some truth about the good is known, but in which there is no power to choose or to achieve what is truly good. That power only comes by the regenerating action of God's grace.

Calvin is neither a determinist nor a fatalist in the way those terms are used now. He is not trying to explain all human action through divine determinism. But, like Augustine and Luther, he is exceedingly careful not to acknowledge any human initiative or power in salvation. For once that allowance is made, however modestly and with whatever good intent, then God's power is limited by human decision. If a person rejects the offer of salvation, then God is powerless to overrule. That kind of limitation on God was completely unthinkable to the Reformers. But it is not so unthinkable today as we shall see later in this chapter.

63

5. Jonathan Edwards

Remaining in the Calvinist tradition we move from the sixteenth to the eighteenth century. Jonathan Edwards, the eminent New England theologian, took up the question of the freedom of the will in a major book bearing that title. Edwards was greatly influenced by the empiricist philosophy of John Locke. It is also striking that Edwards constructs his argument as much like those of some of the modern philosophical determinists we examined earlier, Joynson, Scribner, Franklin, and Smith. The purpose of his essay is to show that causality governs the will as well as all other things.

Edwards defines the will as the power of choice, in the usual, common-sense manner. He then argues that motives determine the will. Motives refer to judgments about the greatest apparent good at the moment of decision. It is necessary that the will act in such a way that this greatest good is achieved.

Edwards then distinguishes between natural and moral necessity "By natural necessity, as applied to men, I mean such necessity as men are under through the force of natural causes; as distinguished from what are called moral causes, such as habits and dispositions of the heart, and moral motives and inducements.[81] Edwards argues that moral necessity may be just as absolute as natural necessity, that is, its effects may be as perfectly connected with moral causes as is a naturally necessary effect with its natural causes. He examines cases of moral inability, and defines two classes of such cases.

> "By a general and habitual moral inability, I mean an
> inability in the heart to all exercises or acts of
> wills of that nature or kind, through a fixed and
> habitual inclination, or an habitual and stated defect,
> or want of a certain kind of inclination. Thus, a very
> ill-natured man may be unable to exercise such acts of
> benevolence, as another, who is full of good nature,
> commonly exerts. ...by particular and occasional moral
> inability, I mean an inability of the will or heart to
> a particular act, through the strength or defect of
> present motives, or of inducements presented to the view
> of the understanding, on this occasion."[82]

So, Edwards argues, it is not, after all, a question of moral ability, but of moral will.

> "Therefore, in these things to ascribe a non-
> performance to the want of power or ability, is not
> just; because the thing wanted is not being able,
> but being willing. There are faculties of mind,

and capacity of nature, and everything else,
sufficient, but a disposition: nothing is
wanting but a will."[83]

As with Calvin, so also with Edwards there is an important connection between the understanding and the will.

"...every act of the will is some way connected with
the understanding, and is as the greatest apparent good
is, in the manner which has already been explained;
namely, that the soul always wills or chooses that
which, in the present view of the mind, considering
in the whole of that view, and all that belongs to
it, appears most agreeable."[84]

These understandings in the mind regarding what is the best are called
motives, and "...if every act of the will is excited by a motive, then
that motive is the cause of the act of the will."[85] In this way, moral
acts are as fully determined as natural acts, since motives themselves
must have some first cause, which is God. So the wills of moral agents
are not truly free wills.

Like Augustine and Calvin, Edwards argues that sin is morally
necessary, natural occurrences are naturally necessary. But by
distinguishing between natural and moral necessity, Edwards can still
assign the blame for sin to humanity, not God. Natural necessity would
make it absurd and unjust to blame or praise human beings for what
they do. Edwards says:

"...if there be an approach to a moral necessity in a
man's exertion of good acts of will, they would be the
exercise of a strong propensity to good, and a very
powerful love of virtue; 'tis so far from being the
dictate of common sense, that he is less virtuous, and
less to be esteemed, loved and praised; than 'tis
agreeable to the natural notions of all mankind that
he is so much the better man, worthy of greater respect,
and higher commendation. And the stronger the inclina-
tion is, and the nearer it approaches to necessity in
that respect, or to impossibility of neglecting the
virtuous act, or of doing a vicious one; still the
more virtuous, and worthy of higher commendations."[86]

That seems to clinch the argument for Edwards. Even common sense shows
that the more habitual (predictable, caused) the virtue, the more we
praise it.

Edward concludes his argument in this way:

"Hereby it becomes manifest, that God's moral
government over mankind, his treating them as moral
agents, making them the objects of his commands, counsels,
calls, warnings, expostulations, promises, threatenings,
rewards and punishments, is not inconsistent with a
determining disposal of all events, of every kind,
throughout the universe, in His providence; either by
positive efficiency, or permission. Indeed, such an
universal, determining providence, infers some kind
of necessity of all events; such a necessity as implies
an infallible previous fixedness of the futurity of the
event: but no other necessity of moral events, or
volitions of intelligent agents, is needful in order
to this, than moral necessity; which does as much
ascertain the futurity of the event, as any other
necessity. But, as has been demonstrated, such a
necessity is not at all repugnant to moral agency,
and the reasonable use of commands, calls, rewards,
punishments, etc."87

Edwards thus carries the doctrine of God's determining power
to its logical conclusion. God truly and literally becomes the only
ultimate cause that there is. Everything else, events in the natural
world and moral decisions, can finally be traced back through their
distinct causal relationships to divine agency.

One could argue that Edwards has simply pushed Pauline-
Augustinian-Calvinist themes to their logical (and absurd) extremity.
Indeed he is trying to maintain (against his Arminiam opponents) an
absolute, radical human dependence upon God's grace for salvation.

But Edwards also thinks in amazingly modern ways. He is in-
sisting that the universe is rationally constructed and governed. So
if we admit that many truly free causal agencies are at work in the
universe, rather than one agency, order and predictability will be
in jeopardy, as well as the gospel.

We conclude our highly selective theological survey of free-
will and determinism with Jonathan Edwards, for not entirely arbitrary
reasons. Modern Western thought (philosophical and scientific as well
as theological) has absorbed the free-will-determinism debate into
characteristically modern categories: mind-body, determinism as a
scientific rather than theological postulate, and the like. Theologians
are no longer the conservators and arbiters of scientific truth. The
Kantian division between the noumenal and phenomenal worlds (roughly,
morals and science) seems to be working well for most people. We
believe in scientific determinism because it has worked well for us
(perhaps too well). At the same time we remain an amazingly fatalistic and superstitious people, believing that God controls the

minute events of our lives. We even attribute the evils we suffer to God (that horrifies us in our more careful and reflective moments) in the belief that there must be some kind of good purpose to be discovered in the midst of evil. And at the same time, we believe in freedom, free choice, free will. And we are especially vigilant about political threats to freedom.

But I do want to outline some conclusions to be drawn from this survey. First, there is the reluctance to affirm human freedom because of the logical consequences - the loss of God and the loss of hope. The existentialist nightmare becomes reality. Humankind is radically alone in the world and condemned to the radical freedom in which there are no objective norms. But if we are not alone in this world - if it is God's world, and if God is the directing and governing agency, then some kind of determinism must be affirmed.

How total or complete must this determinism be? In the tradition we have just surveyed, from the scriptures to Edwards, the movement was clearly toward total determinism. Surely several motives were involved: logical consistency, but also the need to protect God from any responsibility for human evil, while also protecting God's full power and responsibility for human salvation.

But determinism was never a fully satisfactory theological solution to the problem. In these same writers, including Edwards, ways were found to affirm some kind of human free-will.

To what extent do these historic theological treatments of free-will and determinism assist us in making a theological judgment about the truth of behavioral determinism? I will try to show, in the concluding paragraphs of this chapter, how these historic traditions assist us in forming contemporary theological conclusions. But a word is in order about the place of theological tradition in theological construction generally. Any attempt to construct a contemporary theological statement on a pressing human problem must take very seriously the scriptural and theological traditions which may bear upon the problem in question. To "take very seriously" does not mean claiming one particular book or authority as uniquely normative in relation to which others are optional. In the Protestant tradition the scriptures have tended to occupy such a place of unique authority. My faith and Christian life are formed and shaped within that tradition, and that is why I began with scriptural themes. But particularly with a problem like free-will and determinism, the scriptural witnesses speak authoritatively only in the sense that they are the "primary witnesses" (to use Karl Barth's helpful phrase) to the saving events of faith. The scriptures are not themselves capable of yielding a clear or definitive "solution" to an abstractly stated problem such as free-will and determinism. That is why I have relied heavily on major Christian theological thinkers.

67

If "to take very seriously" means something less than
identifying a single normative personage or text, it surely means
something more than simply paging through the past in the search
for confirmations of the conclusions to which one has already
come. The Christian faith and that specialized activity of the
Christian community known as theological construction must always
be seen in its communal character. While we must continually pray
for and wait upon the inspiration of the Holy Spirit to guide our
individual efforts, we can never simply embark upon theological
construction without the discipline of encountering the heritage
of the Christian community through its scriptures, creeds, and
theological teachings. It is in that spirit that I have tried to
conduct this survey, and I trust that it will become clear in the
concluding section of this chapter how this historical inquiry does
indeed shape and mold the conclusions to which I come.

E.   CONCLUSIONS

We began this chapter with the announced intention of raising
and trying to answer the question of the truth of the claim made
by the behaviorists that human behavior is, in principle, predictable
and controllable in a scientific fashion. It may seem that we have
pursued a needlessly involved and round-about route in trying to find
an answer. But I hope to show now that we can weave together some
of the strands of discussion from the behaviorists, from the
philosophy of science and from theology, into a more focused and
coherent statement regarding this problem and its solution.

The key question, it would seem, is whether there is any limit
to behavioral explanation in principle. Neither the behaviorists,
nor their advocates in philosophy and the philosophy of science, nor
other philosophical determinists would argue that a determinist
science has advanced far enough to give a conclusive demonstration
of the truth of behavioral determinism. It becomes, then, at least
for now, a question of belief. Do we believe, must we believe in
the adequacy of the behavioral explanation, even though we cannot
conclusively demonstrate it? Skinner says we must. Other behaviorists
have also said that we must believe in scientific determinism, but
then they turn around and define dimensions of human behavior in
ways that come out looking very much like free-will, free-choice,
intention and purpose.

I want to argue that complete behavioral determinism is an un-
tenable position, but I want also to argue that the difficult task
of understanding and defining the limits of behavioral explanation
does not in any way justify a libertarian position of boundless
freedom. Nor does my attempt to define these limits undermine or

68

demolish a science of human behavior. I will argue that the behavioral sciences, including behaviorism and behavior modification, need to proceed in both research and application on the basis of the belief that highly probable or law-like statements can be derived from a scientific analysis of the human behavior, and that these can be used for predicting and controlling human behavior. And I will argue that such a science ought to proceed with its own conceptual tools and disciplines to extend the boundaries of knowledge as widely as it can. There is nothing about our human dignity, morally or theologically understood, which requires us to establish arbitrary limits on such scientific inquiry.

We must now explore the question on which these conclusions hinge - what it is about human beings that sets limits on the extent of a behaviorally deterministic explanation? I want to propose the thesis that the human qualities which have historically and in common sense language been associated with the term, the will, are the human dimensions which cannot in principle be behaviorally predicted or controlled. In a moment I will attempt to define as carefully and clearly as I can what I mean by the will, but first I want also to suggest that while the question of the adequacy of the behavioral explanation for certain other human qualities cannot be settled either, I do want to acknowledge that the results in behavioral psychology are impressive and promising. To be human is to be constituted of an immensely complex chain of chemical and electrical inter-changes, organized into tissue and organ systems which constitute our human bodies. It appears that with highly probable reliability, scientific studies of these dimensions of the human are capable of high degrees of predictability and controllability. It may prove to be the case that the same high degree of probability holds for the emotions. And although the relationships between thinking and neuro-physiological processes in the brain are not yet well understood, scientific work is advancing in this field.

What do I mean by the will? I have chosen this term in deliberate preference over others which might be clearer or more commonly used. The term ego, from dynamic psychology, may be more widely used and better understood than will. Perhaps it is because will has been associated with the "will-power" of Romantic and Victorian morality, and we are more aware than were our Victorian ancestors of the limitations and distortions of will-power. The ego is a more neutral term, suggesting the functions of maintaining some kind of centering and organizing function among the dynamic elements of the personality, and as the person interacts with events and forces in the environment. Intention, purpose and choice also seem to belong to the ego functions.

I would suggest that ego tends to be a roughly equivalent modern word for the dimensions of human experience which I want to assign to

the will. I prefer will however, because of some of the common-sense
and ancient meanings which appear in the theological texts which were
examined in the previous section.

Another term which might have been used is the self. The self
is a less technical term than ego. Unlike the will and ego, however,
the concept of the self is too broad and inclusive for the purposes
of this analysis. Ordinarily the self includes all that I am aware
of that I identify as a part of "me" and as distinct from everything
which is "not me." Such a definition thus includes everything that
happens in my own body, in my emotions, in my thinking, as well as in
my choosing and deciding. A great deal of what I include under the
concept of my self therefore, seems to fall under the operation of
causality or determination. The way my body and its parts function -
all of these are parts of myself, and yet are not subject to the
administrative activity of the ego or the dictates of the will, except
in very indirect ways specified below.

Ego might suffice were it not so associated with modern psychodynamic psychology. Self is simply too broad and inclusive. Other
concepts might be selected or constructed - Tillich's centered self
(too technical philosophically), conscious awareness (too passive and
cognitive), intentionality (too limited), Frankl's noetic dimension
(overly encumbered philosophically). None of them, it seems to me,
serve as well as simply as the will.

Having, in spite of these alternatives and difficulties, decided
to stay with the will as the best concept for that part of human
experience which cannot in principle be behaviorally predicted and
controlled, I want to define the will more precisely and systematically
by specifying five constituent functions of the will: choice, intention, valuing, character or predisposition, and administration.

We all experience situations of choice, many times each day, in
which we not only feel free but believe that we can choose, without
requiring any further proof that we can. To be sure, certain choices
are easier than others. Some are so highly probable, given our
established habits and the things believe most deeply, that the chances
of doing otherwise are slim. But we still would insist, rightly so,
that these are real choices, not psuedo-choices.

Another function of the will is intention. Experience confirms
that fact that we form intentions somewhere in the mind or conscious
awareness, and then we carry them out in action. We do not carry
out every intention we consider. And we encounter difficulties in
accomplishing our intended objectives. We struggle against limits
and misfortunes. Sometimes we must rethink our intentions and
abandon those which prove to be beyond our ability to accomplish.
But all of that process of struggle and reexamination is involved

in the intentional process, and therefore a part of the will. As with the process of choosing, we are also aware that there are many predisposing or predetermining factors at work in shaping our intentions. We select intentions which experience and sound judgment suggest are within the realm of possibility. The most consuming zeal or ludicrous fantasies eventually soften under the impact of repeatedly frustrated intentions, either from limited resources or abilities. And often we experience that frustrating sense of being caught in situations where whatever we may intend, the outcome seems to be predetermined. The power of the will as intention seems threatened indeed in the struggles of persons who want desperately to change because something in their own personalities, or something in their relationships or their circumstances may be persistently painful and destructive, but who cannot change or escape. The strongest intention cannot produce food for the starving or liberation for the oppressed. Such helplessness does eventually lead to a loss of will or passivity. A great many people are trapped in such frightful circumstances throughout their lives. Most of us have had some taste of such helplessness. But always we hope or wait for something better, which involves the kind of life where intentions can be put into practice. So intention remains a constitutive function of the will, even where desperate circumstances preclude its exercise.

A third function of the will is the process of valuing. Valuing is a modern term, preferred because it covers both decisions and predispositions, and because it does not specify a "correct" set of values. What we come to value and the way our values shape our decisions are dimensions of the will. To a great extent, of course, our values are determined for us. We value what our parents valued, what our culture and immediate social system value, whatever is valued by our families and friends, by the people with whom we work. We do not simply choose or make up our own values. But we do select among options. We decide to what degree we will live by our parental values. We decide about the kind of groups we want to be in, the people we want to work with, the kind of persons we choose for friends or marriage. We decide whether to stay in a particular social system or to undertake a painful or risky transfer into another. And when we face major crises and turning points in life, we try to decide how our basic values shape our response. So even when we become painfully aware of how determined and limited the value choices may be, we still affirm our own responsibility for choosing and living by our values.

A fourth function of the will can be characterized by words like character, disposition, or habit. This function may seem least likely to be properly included with the will, because so many of the things we usually mean by character or disposition are determined by genetic and environmental influences. Psychological and neurophysiological studies of that elusive quality, "temperament," suggest

71

that there are elements of genetic predisposition or very early
(intra-uterine or infancy) environmental influences which establish
a basic quality of organic activity which persists throughout the
life of the individual, little changed by experience. Even if we
do not assign temperament or disposition to genetic and very early
environmental shaping, by the end of childhood or certainly in the
formative period of adolescence, a basic "character," or set of dispositions and habits takes shape, which persists throughout life,
largely impervious to education, vocation, living styles and places,
illness, accident, or failure. It has been widely observed that only
a severe mental breakdown or a radically transforming religious
experience is likely to change these characteristics very much. With
all those good reasons for not ascribing character or temperament to
the will, I still want to argue that there are critical periods and
events in the process of the formation of character or disposition
in which the individual does make extremely important decisions.
These choices may have to do with activities which are to be dropped
in favor of others, new friends to be cultivated in the place of old,
decisions about "what kind of person I really want to be," decisions
about what I believe most deeply and how my life reflects those beliefs, and decisions about changes I must make in order to avoid a
bad outcome. My character is not only formed out of a pattern of
repeated activities and habits. Character is also formed as these
patterns are intersected in moments of reflection and decision. New
life paths are chosen, and new habit patterns are formed, which, in
time do become as deeply constitutive of character as were the former
habit patterns.

The fifth and final function of the will is administration.
Whether one looks to John Calvin or modern ego psychology, it is
commonly believed that the will functions within the conflicts of
dynamic dimensions of the personality, achieving workable compromises
among thinking, feeling and social demands, to enable the personality
to remain acceptably integrated internally and within the social
system. This mediating or administering function of the will grows
and develops as part of the process of individual maturation. Where
these functions are poorly carried out, we have a person who is
either torn by internal conflicts or engaged in conflict with society.
Perfect internal and external harmony are not, however, the norms
for this function of the will. There are many situations in which
such harmony would be out of place, such as destructive and repressive
social environments, or in persons who have experienced destructive
interpersonal relationships covered over by a superficial facade of
harmony. But even though we cannot posit a perfect internal and
external harmony as the norm for the perfect will, we do make judgments
about a sufficient degree of the will's administering capacity for
given persons in given circumstances. People who seek psychotherapy
or are advised to do so often speak of being unable "to manage,"
which phrase suggests insufficient administration. (They may really

want to be "in control," of course, in which case therapy consists of learning to renounce such pretentions of divinity).

I have proposed a definition of the will which includes choosing, intending, valuing, habituating and administering functions. I am arguing that these dimensions of human experience can never be fully or adequately explained by a deterministic behaviorism. To make that case, I next want to describe how the will is formed in a person, what it means to speak of a weak or strong will, how the will may fail to develop fully, or be lost, or destroyed.

The will is formed as the growing child develops the psycho-biological capacities to choose, intend, value, form habits and take responsibility for administration, in social settings (families, peers, schools) where such functions are encouraged--where real choices are offered, and persons held accountable for their choices. Customs and laws in most societies provide a graded set of such experiences for the growing child.

But we discover that in some persons this development is thwarted or dangerously incomplete. Can we understand the causes for this failed development? Some social environments are so controlled and controlling that real choices are never given, or the consequences of choices are never allowed to matter. The result is an abjectly passive person, who might in earlier times have been called "weak-willed," someone who is unable to make decisions, form intentions, act upon them, and live with the consequences. Psychologically such persons are described as having weak egos or poor ego-boundary forma-tion. In some instances, it appears that people who never acquire a relatively consistent and stable pattern of character or disposition may be diagnosed as schizophrenic, or having multiple personalities. They are invaded by alien selfs or fragments of selves - terrifying thoughts and feelings--which do not cohere in any meaningful way. And there is a kind of failure to form the will which may be expressed as a breakdown in the administering function, either in the form of being unable to reconcile instinctual and social demands, as in the cases of the more severe psychoneuroses and psychoses, or in those diagnosed as sociopaths or psychopaths, who have never successfully integrated into their own character the norms and values of family, social system, or culture. So every requirement of society is viewed as an alien demand, which is actively opposed or violated, by irra-tional assaults on persons or property.

Unfortunately we do not understand why the will has failed to form or taken a destructive turn in many individual cases. But if my argument is sound, we should look for experiences where choices were not given, or where responsibility was not taken and required.

Short of these obvious pathologies of the will, within a broadly

73

normal range of human experience, one can posit a continuum from weak-willed to strong-willed persons. The language of common sense is full of such references. We all know people we would call weak-willed, who are easily led astray from their professed values, who find it difficult to make choices and who postpone choices as long as they can, who apparently must expend great effort to mediate between internal and external demands, persons who seem to be constantly at war with themselves and with others, persons who form ambitious or fanciful intentions but can never carry them out. And, similarly, we know persons whom we call "strong-willed," whose lives reflect consistent patterns of disposition and habit. They are more predictable than our weak-willed friends. They formulate intentions and usually carry them out. Sometimes these intentions emerge in childhood or adolescence, and the rest of life represents the unfolding of a basic plan. They know what they value and usually act consistently with those values. Their internal and external conflicts are handled with a minimal amount of difficulty. Sometimes these strong-willed people are judged stubborn, rigid, or compulsive, if they cannot negotiate, relax, or be playfully spontaneous.

Just as we can describe the formation of the will, and weak and strong wills, we can identify ways in which a developed will can be strengthened, weakened, or destroyed. The will is strengthened when it is employed. But how does that process begin? There must be a conducive environment. Real choices must be given and responsibility required. There must also be love-consistent, committed, positive regard. But there appears to be also a decision, an act of the will which only the person can make, to consider choices and take responsibility, to receive love. No matter how warmly supportive the relationships, there is no guarantee that love and sound moral instruction will prevail on their own. There must be receptivity, acquiescence, decision, acts of will. It is like the decision a person makes to undertake psychotherapy, or to pursue further education. Without such an initial act of will, the prospects for therapy or education are poor. So while we can describe the kinds of experiences and relationships in which the will develops and is strengthened, we cannot control or manage that process environmentally. The person must give consent, which indicates that the will already exists and is functioning.

If consent is given, educational or therapeutic experiences can be provided which develop and strengthen the functions of the will. Wise parents and teachers have always sensed how to blend support and challenge in the right proportion for the child's growing will.

And just as experiences can be provided which strengthen the will, it is also possible to devise procedures for weakening and destroying the will -- where choices are not given, love is unreal or inconsistent, intentions are irrationally frustrated, and the efforts at integration and administration by the will are undermined. Some examples would be political coercion and control, brain-washing, torture, and the deliberate manipulation of relationships and environments to produce passivity, confusion, and hopelessness. All relationships and social systems have elements of these will-destroying dynamics. Politically repressive systems make a more deliberate and conscious use of them. In marriages and family relationships there are often frighteningly effective physical or psychological measures to weaken or destroy the wills of dissident spouses or children. Judgments about the health or humaneness of a society or family are made on the basis of how well the system facilitates or inhibits the growth and exercise of the wills of its members.

So far I have argued that the will is constitutive of any fully developed human personality; there are ways in which the will grows and is strengthened; and there are ways in which the will is weakened and destroyed. But I have also argued that none of our ways of nurturing the will can produce it. Only by consent, by decision, which is an act of will, can a person profit from love, guidance, challenge and increased freedom.

While the will must already be "there," at least in sufficient strength to give consent, there are further conditions to be specified if the will is to develop sufficiently. These are the organic capacities required to bear the activities of choosing, intending, valuing, character-forming and administering. These organic capacities are centered in the organs of sense and the brain.

The connection between will and reason was noted by Augustine, Aquinas, Calvin and Edwards. If a person is genetically or environmentally deficient in the ability to think and reason, then the functions of the will are diminished by the degree of that deficiency. That is why, in custom and in law, we do not regard severely mentally retarded persons as responsible for the consequences of their actions. They do not possess the mental ability required to reflect and choose wisely.

But thinking does not depend only on mental capacity. Perceptual abilities and limitations affect the power of thought and thus the will. Studies of persons born blind or deaf suggest that such limits do affect thinking, and thus the will. Feelings strongly affect what we perceive and what we think about what we perceive. That is undoubtedly one of the reasons why an emotionally corrective experience like psychotherapy may be a prerequisite for the kind of clearer thinking that is required for strengthening the will.

So far, I have tried to define the human will by its functions, to describe its formation, to characterize the experiences in which the will is either strengthened or weakened, and to discuss some of the necessary conditions for the existence of a functional will. I have relied on the language of common-sense observation, along with certain concepts from psychology and psychotherapy. But I have argued all along that the fundamental case for such an understanding of the will is theological in character. So I now want to return to the theological survey which appeared in this chapter, in order to show that this notion of the will does indeed represent that theological tradition.

We observed that the theologians all found some way, awkward and complex though it might be, to affirm some kind of free will. Gregory of Nyssa would extend human freedom to include the freedom which the person has to believe or reject the Gospel. The Augustinian and Reformed traditions affirm a more limited but still genuine freedom, in which free-will could be decisively exercised only by choosing to rebel against God, but people could not freely choose salvation without the aid of divine grace. The Augustinian and Reformed traditions found ways, however, to affirm domains of free-will not lost or corrupted by the fall.

Even Jonathan Edwards, who more than all the rest sought to uphold the doctrine of a determined world against what he judged to be the chaotic indeterminism of the Arminians, still provided for distinctions between natural and moral necessity, so that determinism could not be seen as fatalism. I have emphasized the Augustinian, Calvinist and Edwardian dimensions of this Western theological tradition because they are generally regarded the most extreme advocates of divine determinism and consequent human helplessness. But even they have been compelled to find ways to account for a free human will.

A second central theme in this theological tradition is the two-fold determining power of God, determining for human salvation, since God's graciousness is required to be saved from the deserved punishment, but also determining in the sense that God's creating and sustaining will is at work in all things. These saving and sustaining determinations can never be fully understood, even by the faith-enlightened person. But there is a clear sense that God's determination is what gives our world of experience the order and meaning which it inherently possesses, that these determinations shape our lives, and thus limit the domain of human freedom, but that these limits do not reduce humanity to something without a deliberative will that is free to choose and act. However darkened and weakened by sin the will may be, it continues to exist as a constitutive part of humankind.

A third theme which appears in this Western theological tradition is that of the evil will and the good will. The evil will is oriented to some kind of idolatry in which something other than God is placed at the center of life. The good will is a will which has been reoriented, or transformed by God's grace, and becomes a will which is trusting, faithful, righteous, directed to good works. The same parts of the personality are still there--reason, feelings, and the like, but now the centering or administering character of the will has organized all these parts into a new configuration which orients them to God, rather than to the lesser gods which may have been served before.

I would suggest that what the dominant Western theological tradition has meant by an evil will is functionally equivalent to the descriptions of a weak or lost will from common-sense observation and psychology. To be fallen theologically is to be weak-filled. We do not know how to make decisions, what intentions are worthy and what are unworthy, what to value at the center of our lives, what sort of character or disposition to nourish, and how to mediate between conflicts within and without. Thus salvation does not mean more knowledge or information for the mind, and salvation does not mean therapy for the emotions or the body. Salvation finally consists of a strengthening reorientation in the will. Since the will is the choosing, intending, valuing, character-forming and administering agency of the human person, the transformed will in salvation has effects throughout the personality. Thinking is clarified. Feelings become enlivening rather than menacing. The body functions in more integrated and healthy ways. But no one of these other dimensions of life is as central to salvation, as is the will.

A fourth theme in this Western theological tradition is the fundamental conflict over whether people are free to reject the gift of salvation. The scriptures and early theologians like Gregory of Nyssa say that they are. But the Augustinian-Reformed strand of tradition says they are not. Are any really crucial matters at stake in this dispute? The Augustinian-Reformed tradition has not wanted to admit any limit upon God's power, for fear that God would become one among many variously powerful forces at work. And so salvation might not ever be fully assured.

But that assurance has been purchased at a frightful price: a god of sovereign power who must therefore bear some responsibility for evil; and a humankind unable to will or choose its own good. So I believe we are on better ground to risk some lack of assurance about our own ultimate destiny by affirming the freedom of the will to reject the gift of salvation. The call of Christ in the Gospels to repent and believe surely means that there is a critical point of decision at which one must say yes or no for oneself. I would suggest that this critical point in hearing the good news of God's grace and claiming it for one's self is analogous to that critical point described earlier, in which one must decide to act on choices,

receive love, or begin some therapeutic or educational experience
to deal with difficulties and strengthen the will. Much of what
follows may be determined. But first there is a decision which must
be made by the person, which is not caused or determined by existing
circumstances, even by the divine initiative in offering the grace
which is required for salvation.

I have suggested that the fallen will understood theologically
corresponds to the weak will understood psychologically, and that
the transforming reorientation of the will similarly corresponds to
what was discussed psychologically as the strengthening of the will.
Identifying this striking theological correspondence is not intended
to prove the claims of faith, nor is it intended to de-value a non-
theological understanding of the will. But faith claims do continually
press for experiential confirmation, and reach out for resonance in
common human experience. This analysis of the will seems a clear
example of such resonance.

We now conclude this chapter by discussing the implications of
this theological-psychological understanding of the will for behavioral
determinism and behavior modification, specifically for the question
of the truth of the behavioral claim to be able to explain, predict
and control. I would argue that there are four crucial implications.
First, behaviorism and behavior modification require that we take
more seriously all the ways in which human behavior can be explained,
predicted and controlled. As modern heirs of the Enlightenment, in
a culture affirming freedom and dignity, we all attribute a great
deal more to human freedom than we should. Skinner is quite right
in ridiculing the absurd lengths to which we go to maintain a human-
centered view of the universe. But we surely do not need to succumb
to environmental determinism to recognize the extent and the depth
of the environmental and genetic determinations which shape our lives.
There are reasons short of the claims of a deterministic science or
a deterministic Calvinism for acknowledging the ways we are determined.
These reasons can be discovered in the depths of our own hearts, as
we struggle with very modest changes we want to make, changes we know
we should make -- in our own personal lives, in our closest relationships, in the institutional and social roles we occupy--only to find
that our past "histories of reinforcement" are inscribed there in
the very center of our being, and we are not free.

I do not sense that my colleagues in the Christian community,
particularly in the disciplines of theology or therapeutic psychology,
want to confront the extent of such determination. Rather, I seem
constantly to encounter a blandly cheerful optimism about the
possibilities for change born of the marriage between "human potential"
psychology and personalistic piety. A greater immersion in Calvin
and Skinner would do them all a great deal of good.

Secondly, behaviorism cannot now, or ever, explain the operations of the will in a deterministic fashion. The behavioral psychologists should, however, continue to search for explanations for choosing, intending, valuing and the like. And surely the will is influenced by biological and environmental forces. But I have argued that there are key decisional events and processes which are uniquely characteristic of the human will and which cannot in principle be scientifically explained, predicted or controlled.

What actually happens then, when environmentally powerful influences are applied to changing the will? They can be effective in only one of two ways: either the person gives consent, or the will is deliberately weakened or destroyed. The will cannot be seduced, even by the positive reinforcements of a *Walden Two*. People might consent to enter such an environment. And they might find that it does weaken the will--choices and difficulties are diminished or removed. But since people consented to enter that environment, they can always decide to leave, unless forcibly detained. So the controllers will not be able to take over by positive reinforcement alone. We will have to let them. And even the happiest slaves retain the memory and hope of freedom.

Thirdly, it follows from what was just said, that while we will not be seduced unaware into a behaviorally controlled social order, we do need to exercise extreme care about using behavioral methods on unwilling subjects. What often really happens is not that behavior modification has worked, but behavioral methods are used to weaken or destroy the will, in a more refined and subtle ways than with more obviously coercive measures. While there may be management gains to be obtained through weakening or breaking the wills of persons, such violence seems hardly ever justified. These questions of the ethics of behavior modification will be explored more fully in the next chapter.

Fourth, while I have argued that the will cannot be explained, predicted or controlled behaviorally, I believe we should support the kind of work in basic behavioral science and in the philosophy of behavioral science which seeks to create and refine unitary concepts of science rather than fundamentally dualistic concepts. Every effort should be made in such a unitary scientific framework to find the language and develop the principles by which the activities of the will can be described and explained in the same way in which other phenomena are studied. If the activities of the will are not capable of being scientifically understood with the precision of law-like statements, we would still be immeasurably helped in our understanding to arrive at statements of high probability.

Is it, then, true? Can a deterministic behaviorism explain, predict and control human behavior? Part of the answer to that question can only be given at some future time, when the concepts and methods

of behavioral science have been further developed. But part of the
answer can be given now: so far as any human being possesses a will,
up to that limit the behavioral explanation may be more adequate than
others; beyond that limit, the behavioral explanation can illumine
but never explain. Behaviorism will help us to understand with
greater percision how the will is influenced, and what kind of
experiences weaken or strengthen the will. But behaviorism cannot
ever explain or predict or control the outcomes of the functions of
the will--choosing, intending, valuing, character forming and administering.

NOTES FOR CHAPTER III

[1] B. F. Skinner, *Science and Human Behavior* (New York: MacMillan,
1953), 5.

[2] B. F. Skinner, *Walden Two* (New York: MacMillan, 1948), 263.

[3] *Ibid.*, 296-297.

[4] B. F. Skinner, *About Behaviorism* (New York: Random House, 1974),
217.

[5] *Walden Two*, 264.

[6] *Ibid.*, 289.

[7] B. F. Skinner, *Beyond Freedom and Dignity* (New York: Knopf, 1971),
163.

[8] *About Behaviorism*, 211.

[9] Leonard Krasner, *Journal of Social Issues*, April, 1965, 12.

[10] *Ibid.*, 23.

[11] *Ibid.*, 24.

[12] Leonard Krasner, "Behavior Modification - Values and Training: The
Perspective of Psychologist," in *Behavior Therapy: Appraisal and
Status*, ed. by Cyril M. Franks (New York: McGraw-Hill, 1969),
550-551.

[13]W. Edward Craighead, Alan E. Kazdin, Michael J. Mahoney, *Behavior Modification. Principles, Issues, and Application* (Boston: Houghton - Mifflin, 1976), 172.

[14]*Ibid.*, 174.

[15]*Ibid.*

[16]*Ibid.*, 175.

[17]*Ibid.*

[18]*Ibid.*, 178.

[19]Kanfer and Keroly, "Self-Control: A Behavioristic Excursion into the Lion's Den," *Behavior Therapy*, 3 (1972), 412-413.

[20]*Ibid.*, 407.

[21]*Ibid.*, 410-411.

[22]Edward D'Angelo, *The Problem of Freedom and Determinism* (Columbia, Missouri: University of Missouri Press, 1968), 1.

[23]William James. "The Dilemma of Determinism," in *The Will to Believe and Other Essays* (New York: Dover Press, 1956), 152-153.

[24]*Ibid.*, 161-162.

[25]*Ibid.*, 171.

[26]*Ibid.*, 174-175.

[27]*Ibid.*, 176-177.

[28]*Ibid.*, 177.

[29]*Ibid.*, 180-181.

[30]*Minnesota Studies in the Philosophy of Science*, Vol. II, ed. by Herbert Feigl, Michael Scrive, Grover Maxwell (Minneapolis: University of Minnesota Press, 1958), 332.

[31]*Ibid.*, 426.

[32]*Ibid.*, 429.

[33]*Ibid.*, 432.

[34]*Ibid.*, 460-461.

[35]Sigmund Koch, "Psychology and Emergency Conceptions of Knowledge as Unitary," in *Behaviorism and Phenomenology*, ed. by T. W. Wann (Chicago: University of Chicago Press, 1964), 6.

[36]G. E. M. Auscombe, *Causality and Determinism* (London: Cambridge University Press, 1971), 28.

[37]W. E. Hocking, *The Self: Its Body and Freedom* (New Haven: Yale University Press, 1978), 153.

[38]William H. Davis, *The Freewill Question* (The Hague: M. Nijhoff, 1971), 39.

[39]*Ibid.*, 43.

[40]*Ibid.*, 77.

[41]Austin Farrer, *The Freedom of the Will* (London: Adam and Charles Blacke, 1958), 235.

[42]R. B. Joynson, *Psychology and Common Sense* (London: Routledge and Kegan Paul, 1974), 68.

[43]Phillip H. Scribner, "Accounting for the Failure of Behaviorism" in *Explanation: New Directions in Philosophy* (The Hague: M. Nijhoff, 1973).

[44]R. L. Franklin, *Freewill and Determinism* (London: Routledge and Kegan Paul, 1968), 304-305.

[45]Kendon Smith, *Behavior and Conscious Experience, A Conceptual Analysis* (Athens Ohio: Ohio University Press, 1969), 129-130.

[46]Norman Malcom, "Behaviorism as a Philosophy of Psychology," in *Behaviorism and Phenomenology*, 150.

[47] *Ibid.*

[48] *Ibid.*, 153.

[49] *Ibid.*, 154.

[50] Charles Taylor, "Interpretation and the Sciences of Man." *The Review of Metaphysics*, Sept., 1971, XXV, No. 1, 3-51.

[51] George Mandler and William Kerson, "The Appearance of Free Will," *Philosophy of Psychology*, ed. S. C. Broom (London: MacMillan, 1974), 317.

[52] Howard W. Hintz, "Whitehead's Concept of Organism," in *Dimensions of Mind*, ed. by Sydney Hook. (New York: University Press, 1960), 104.

[53] Gregory of Nyssa, "The Great Catechism" in *Nicene and Post Nicene Fathers of the Christian Church*, Second Series Vol. 5, (Grand Rapids: Wm. B. Eerdmans, 1954), 479.

[54] *Ibid.*, 499.

[55] Augustine of Hippo, The Retractions, The Fathers of the Church, Vol. 60, (Washington: The Catholic University of America Press, 1968), 35.

[56] *Ibid.*, 36.

[57] Augustine of Hippo, "On Grace and Free Will," *Nicene and Post Nicene Fathers*, First Series, Vol. 5 (Grand Rapids: Wm. B. Eerdmans, 1956), 456.

[58] *Ibid.*, 457.

[59] *Ibid.*, 458.

[60] Thomas Aquinas, "Of Divine Providence," *The Library of Christian Classics*, Vol. XI, *Nature and Grace* (Phildelphia: The Westminster Press, 1954), 97.

[61] *Ibid.*, 100.

[62]*Ibid.*, 112.

[63]St. Thomas Aquinas, *Theological Texts*, ed. Thomas Gilby (London: Oxford University Press, 1955), 99.

[64]St. Thomas Aquinas, *Philosophical Texts*, ed. Thomas Gilby (London: Oxford University Press, 1951), 261-262.

[65]*Ibid.*, 109.

[66]*Ibid.*, 119.

[67]Martin Luther, *The Bondage of the Will*, ed. & trans. by J. I. Packer and O. R. Johnston (New York: Fleming H. Revell Company, 1957), 107.

[68]*Ibid.*, 137.

[69]John Calvin, *Institutes of the Christian Religion*, Vol. I, trans. by John Allen (Philadelphia: Board of Christian Education, 1936), 281.

[70]*Ibid.*

[71]*Ibid.*, 286.

[72]*Ibid.*, 293.

[73]*Ibid.*, 294.

[74]*Ibid.*, 297.

[75]*Ibid.*, 308-309.

[76]*Ibid.*, 318.

[77]*Ibid.*

[78]*Ibid.*, 319.

[79]*Ibid.*, 321.

[80]*Ibid.*, 327.

[81]Jonathan Edwards, *Freedom of the Will*, ed. Paul Ramsey (New Haven: Yale University Press, 1957), 156-157.

[82]*Ibid.*, 160.

[83]*Ibid.*, 162.

[84]*Ibid.*, 217.

[85]*Ibid.*, 225.

[86]*Ibid.*, 360.

[87]*Ibid.*, 431.

CHAPTER IV

THE ETHICS OF BEHAVIOR MODIFICATION

In this chapter we will try to determine who may employ behavior modifying procedures to treat what kinds of persons under what circumstances. These are important questions for society to face, but particularly so by those who might use behavior modification, personally or institutionally.

We will examine the ethical outlook of B. F. Skinner and other behaviorists. Then we shall examine some cases where behavior modification has been or might be used. I will try to show how appropriate ethical guidelines might be used in such cases. But first we will need to look at the character of ethical thinking and deciding.

A. ETHICAL THINKING AND DECIDING

I begin by observing that there is a pervasive mood in our society which regards ethics as the same as private, personal and subjective preferences. This relegation of ethics to the domain of private values leads to the sense that there is no worth in public and social ethical discourse, since what we finally fall back on is our subjective preferences. Along with this minimal definition of ethics is the view that we should attempt to maximize opportunities for individuals to express and act on their subjective and personal value orientations with the least amount of social prohibition and interference consistent with the maintenance of the social good. But once considerations of social welfare are introduced, we have in fact entered the realm of public ethical discourse, requiring that we conduct this discourse according to socially approved ethical norms and principles.

We must certainly acknowledge the importance of the subjective and private side of ethics. We have gained (and should not ever lose) the recognition that no single system of beliefs and ethics can be allowed to control customs and laws in a pluralistic society. But while society must protect the private and subjective dimension of ethical decisions, society also requires that there be norms and procedures for determining right and wrong, which all members of society uphold. While we may be living in a period during which the

87

traditional sources of moral authority and decision-making are considerably weakened, it is simply not true that collective moral and
ethical decisions are no longer being faced or made.

Ethical reflection and decision-making in behavior modification
occur all the time: in discussions conducted by psychologists and
professionals engaged in the application of psychological knowledge;
in the formation of professional ethics, and in the process of creating
mechanisms for monitoring the observation of codes of ethical practice;
when laws, regulations and guidelines are adopted by public bodies
of all levels of our society; and in the discussions of the applications
of behavior modification which appear in the mass media.

There are three kinds of elements necessary for truly useful
ethical reflection and decision-making on public policy questions such
as behavior modification. The first element is some kind of normative
vision. In the traditional religious systems, this normative vision
could be expressed in rules or teachings (the Ten Commandments, the
Sermon on the Mount) which were believed to summarize the will of God.
Or this normative vision might also be stated in the images of some
perfect social system or world order which was given both as a goal
toward which people ought to work, and also as the vision of the
perfected age--which would appear only when God acts to create a
perfect human community out of the imperfect human communities of
history. Examples of such images of the perfect human community
abound in the scriptures of Judaism and Christianity - the Messianic
Age, a time of harmony among human beings and between humanity and
nature, the kingdom of God, the new Jerusalem as a heavenly city,
and the like.

But there are also normative visions expressed in rules of conduct or descriptions of the ideal social order which are not based
upon a particular religious belief-system. There are normative images
based upon philosophical convictions about the good life. These
visions may be represented through philosophical and moral explorations
of the character of human justice, or an understanding of what human
beings most need in order to achieve the greatest realization of their
capacities. There are also secular utopias which depict an ideal
state of affairs in which harmony, justice and the greatest opportunities for individual growth and achievement are all attained. In
our own time, these secular utopias have reflected the values which
we prize in an age of human rights and scientific-technological progress
such as freedom from want, from ignorance, from disease, from social
and political oppression, and freedom for the achievement of individual
creative potentialities employed in the service of a more humane
social order.

Whether ethical thinking is based on traditional religious
formulations, or on philosophically or scientifically grounded beliefs,

all ethical thinking finally requires some such vision or some set of irreducible beliefs about the human good and the right and wrong ways to attain the human good. These are never static visions. There is an on-going process of testing and refining visions of the good life, as societies confront decisions about new situations which are not readily resolved by reference to the primary vision. One of the problems in the ethics of behavior modification has been the tendency of some behaviorists, particularly Skinner, to assume that a certain vision of the good life (survival, scientific progress, happiness) is the only vision. But in fact such visions are complex; they do change; and they are never so neat and clear-cut as we might assume. Making ethical decisions about behavior modification requires that we engage in a continuing public discourse regarding the most basic ethical foundation of social and personal life, and that we not beg ethical questions by invoking an ethical vision as though it never changed.

The second element required in ethical reflection and decision-making consists of principles or guidelines which are required for bringing abstract statements of moral law or an abstract image of the perfect human community into some kind of useful relationship with specific cases of ethical decision-making. If, for example, it is believed that justice ought to prevail in human relationships, so that each person is treated fairly and impartially, with equal access to life's necessities and opportunities, how do we apply this notion of justice to a specific decision about the use of behavior modification? Some methods of behavior modification employ small but deliberate doses of physical pain. Is it ever just, in order to increase the future social adjustment (and thus happiness) of the patient to employ a method in which an apparently unjust and undeserved application of pain is used? One way of deciding this difficult question is to attempt to show that the losses in human justice suffered in the treatment process are clearly offset by the gains in human justice which can be expected as an outcome of treatment. It is some such procedure of ethical reasoning which is required to translate abstract moral precepts or visions into workable guidelines for ethical decision making about specific cases.

A third element in the process of ethical reflection and decision making in behavior modification would be a sufficient knowledge of the technical details of the uses of behavior modification in therapy, education, or institutional management. Without this foundation in the knowledge of practice, ethical discussion may not be useful. As we shall soon see, there are both advocates and critics of behavior modification who prefer abstract ethical arguments, which fail to take into account the complexities faced in many actual treatment situations where such decisions have to be made.

It should be clear that my own vision of a just human community is theologically grounded in the Christian affirmation that it is the

89

God made known in Jesus Christ who provides the essential vision, and who also provides resources of spirit and will for struggling to realize that vision. But I trust that it will become equally clear that this vision of the justly fulfilled human community is not the private vision of historic Christianity or any of its branches, but that it shares much in common with modern philosophically and politically grounded visions of the good life which have characterized the aims (if not the attainments) of Western civilization. I make this observation in order to suggest that along with our welcome emphasis on diversity and pluralism, there remains a deep and strong commonality of moral belief in Western culture, which can be appropriately shared by those professing particular religious faiths and those professing none, in the process of examining and making decisions about what is ethical in the application of behavior modification.

This brief sketch of the elements of ethical thinking and deciding will be filled out as we look at the ethical views of behaviorists and as we consider specific cases of application.

B. B. F. SKINNER AS ETHICIST

B. F. Skinner has been preoccupied with ethical and social questions in all of his major writings on the uses of behavior modification. Skinner's ethical thought is difficult to distill and focus, because he so regularly and outrageously mixes statements of presumed fact with statements of value. But one can make out a clear moral vision, which I will try to summarize.

The ultimate good, according to Skinner, is cultural survival. "Survival is the only value according to which a culture is eventually to be judged, and any practice that furthers survival has survival value by definition."[1] It is survival which ultimately determines which things are good and which are bad. "Things are good (positively reinforcing) or bad (negatively reinforcing) presumably because of the contingencies of survival under which the species evolved."[2] Throughout his writings, Skinner refers to himself as an evolutionist and expresses his great indebtedness to Darwin. He also notes that most of his critics have failed to take sufficiently seriously the evoluntionary element in his thinking. But evolutionary theory does not say what ought to be. It simply explains why some species survive and others do not. This is a glaring (but common) error in ethical thinking - to use a descriptive statement (fact) as a moral statement (ought). The implicit reasoning goes something like this: some cultures survive but some do not. We can now understand through behavioral science what kinds of activities promote cultural disintegration and death. We therefore ought to plan and conduct our cultural life in ways that will guarantee our survival rather than our death. It is this movement from "is" to "ought" which poses the greatest difficulty for Skinner's ethical vision. And it is this precise point that has been most searchingly questioned by philosophers and ethicists.

As we noted in the previous chapter, Skinner believes that science is far better than other and more ancient forms of human knowledge. "Science is cumulative and progressive; art, philosophy, poetry and theology are not."[3] Skinner understands science to be composed of three elements: a set of attitudes including the rejection of previous authorities, the willingness to face facts even when facts are opposed to wishes, and the willingness to get along without a definitive or final answer. Secondly, science involves a search for order, for uniformities, for lawful relations among the events in nature. And science involves also the belief that human behavior is not exempt from lawful relations among the events in nature, but rather is different only in terms of its greater complexity.

In addition to emphasizing the accumulative and progressive character of science, Skinner emphasizes the success of science. "The methods of science have been enormously successful wherever they have been tried. Let us then apply them to human affairs."[4] In much of his writing this same theme is sounded, that is, that science is so much more successful in providing sure and certain knowledge for human guidance that we ought to be using it more widely in society, to attain degrees of human improvement which have so far escaped us by more traditional means.

"We find ourselves members of a culture in which science has flourished and in which the methods of science have come to be applied to human behavior. If, as seems to be the case, the culture derives strength from this fact, it is a reasonable prediction that a science of behavior will continue to flourish and that our culture will make a substantial contribution to the social environment of the future."[5]

Because Skinner believes so firmly in the principle of the lawful and predictable character of all events, including human behavior, he argues for a strict determinism, (as we saw in chapter 3). Determinism makes it difficult for him to acknowledge any human agency or choice, which must be assumed if there is to be any ethical decision making at all. Nevertheless, Skinner violates his own strict determinism by engaging in passionate ethical sermonizing, as he calls on his readers to be aware of the peril if they fail to apply science behaviorally, and the promises which await us if they do.

It is this sense of impending doom which helps us understand his moral vision. In *Beyond Freedom and Dignity*, Skinner depicts our contemporary society as one that is hell-bent for destruction, because everyone is going around seeking immediate gratification (behavioral reinforcement), understandable, to be sure, but potentially destructive. Skinner says:

"...the challenge may be answered by intensifying the contingencies which generate behavior for the good of others or by pointing to previously neglected individual gains, such as those conceptualized as security, order, health, wealth, or wisdom."[6]

"The great problems of the world today are all global. Overpopulation, the depletion of resources, the pollution of the environment, and the possibility of a nuclear holocaust - these are the not-so-remote consequences of present courses of action. But pointing to consequences is not enough. We must arrange contingencies under which consequences have an effect. How can the cultures of the world bring these terrifying possibilities to bear on the behavior of their members?"[7]

Skinner advocates the use of behavioral technology to plan for the survival of a culture by reinforcing those actions which work toward the long-range benefit of the culture rather than for the short range reinforcements of individual members of the culture. While the goal of cultural survival is clearly good for Skinner, he argues that behavioral technology itself is neither good nor evil.

"Such a technology is ethically neutral. It can be used by villian or saint. There is nothing in a methodology which determines the values governing its use. We are concerned here, however, not merely with practices, but with the design of a whole culture, and the survival of a culture then emerges as a special kind of value."[8]

So far we have looked at three values in Skinner's ethical thinking: the value of cultural survival; the positive value of science, especially when compared with other human ways of knowing; and the survival value of intentional cultural planning.

Skinner's critics have been quick to identify the loss of human freedom, the reduction of human beings to links in a causal behavioral change, and the possibilities for total social control in the hands of a controlling elite, as key flaws in Skinner's ethical vision.

Skinner is certainly aware of these criticisms, and has tried to deal with them, as we saw in the last chapter, with the concept of countercontrol.

All controlling relationships, according to Skinner, involve reciprocal or mutual dimensions, in which the controller is, at the same time, being controlled by the subject animal, person or population. Thus,

> "...the great problem is to arrange effective counter-control and hence to bring some important consequences to bear on the behavior of the controller. Some classical examples of a lack of balance between control and countercontrol arise when control is delegated and countercontrol then becomes ineffective. Hospitals for psychotics and homes for retardates, orphans, and old people are noted for weak countercontrol, because those who are concerned for the welfare of such people do not know what is happening. Prisons offer little opportunity for countercontrol, as the commonest controlling measures indicate."[9]

In talking about these control situations which are out of balance, Skinner goes on to say:

> "...self-government often seems to solve the problem by identifying the controller with the controls. The principle of making the controller a member of the group he controls should apply to the designer of a culture. ...there is a sense in which a culture controls itself, as a person controls himself...."[10]

In *About Behaviorism*, Skinner says:

> "...countercontrol is no doubt not the only reason why one person treats another person well. We might act in such a way that another person is reinforced and reinforces us in return. The human genetic endowment may include some such tendency.... In any case, the way one person treats another is determined by reciprocal action."[11]

This curious term, countercontrol, goes beyond the more narrow and specialized meaning of control understood in the sense of designing laboratory or therapeutic or institutional arrangements in which the behavior of the subjects can be predicted and managed with precision. In common language, it would seem better to use words like influence or power in expressing what Skinner means. He is talking about the fact that no one, not any researcher or scientist or dictator, has free reign over the persons and things

93

within the manager's sphere of influence. Skinner appears to be suggesting that the more equally such power can be distributed, the better will be the consequences for the individual as well as for the social group. In other words, countercontrol approximates the more familiar principle of the just distribution of power in a democracy.

But there are other places in Skinner's writing where it is clear that he does not mean to have a genuine democratic distribution of power. Rather, it seems that a behaviorally planned society will eliminate the need for checks and balances because the whole society will be arranged in such a way that everyone's needs will be met, and thus there will be no need for punishment or the threat of punishment. This line of thinking is most clearly developed in his Utopian novel, *Walden Two*. In defending his Utopian commune, Frazier, the behavioral manager, says:

> "...this is the freest place on earth. And it is free precisely because we make no use of force or threat of force... by skillful planning, by a wise choice of techniques we increase the feeling of freedom."[12]

In responding to the charge of despotism, Frazier says:

> "...it's a limited sort of despotism... and I don't think anyone should worry about it. The despot must wield his power for the good of others. If he takes any step which reduces the sum total of human happiness, his power is reduced by a like amount. What better check against a malevolent despotism could you ask for?"[13]

Frazier also defends his Utopian despotism with an attack on other forms: "I don't like despotism either! I don't like the despotism of ignorance. I don't like the despotism of neglect, of irresponsibility, the despotism of accident, even. And I don't like the despotism of democracy!"[14] Frazier goes on to say that the despotism of democracy "guaranteed only that the majority will not be despotically ruled."[15] Here Skinner depicts a Utopian state of natural harmony which will replace all present social systems in which power and rewards are imperfectly distributed. With the advent of the behaviorally controlled society, in other words, after a transitional generation has passed, everyone will be happy in a natural sort of way because everyone will want to do what is good for the individual, which is at the same time in harmony with the good for the social community. This kind of reinforcement will presumably overrule the reinforcing consequences of accumulated power, which has been difficult to check throughout human history.

Critics have accused Skinner of being immoral or amoral. I have tried to show that there is a kind of moral vision running through Skinner's philosophical and political writings, a vision which depicts a human community in which survival and growth are possible because decisions have been made about behavior to be reinforced which goes beyond the classical procedures of punishment, threat of punishment, limits on power, and the tendency for each person to work for reinforcements which are immediate and personal, but which may prove to be maladaptive for the future of the culture. I have also tried to indicate that there are critical logical problems running through Skinner's statements about the good society, problems having to do with equating the descriptive theory of evolution and the descriptive power of science with the positive moral good.

Skinner's humanitarian intentions are not to be doubted. He genuinely believes that our culture is heading toward self destruction, and he is trying to argue that applied behavioral technology may save us. And Skinner is certainly not insensitive to the possible misuse of behavior modification by despots who would seek their own limited and selfish purposes, though it is apparent that Skinner believes that such behavior would itself be so negatively reinforced by their subjects that such tyranny could not last.

That is as much allowance as we can make, however, for Skinner as an ethicist. Skinner gives no help at all on ethical guidelines or principles which are required to relate a normative vision to specific social problems and questions of treatment. His philosophical and political writings are at such an abstract and general level, encompassing all of Western civilization and contemporary human society, that we simply cannot derive from them specific judgments about where to begin, with whom, and under what conditions or circumstances. In addition, Skinner does not trouble himself with the technical details of actual situations where behavior modification is being employed. Though he is a brilliant research scientist, when he talks about applied behavior modification he prefers to speculate about grandiose possibilities rather than grappling with applications currently in use or proposed.

But we must take Skinner's vision seriously, since he is our preeminently influential behaviorist, and as we shall see, his ethical ideas have influenced other behaviorists.

C. CRITICISM OF SKINNER AS ETHICIST

Since the publication of _Walden Two_ in 1948, Skinner's utopian vision has been subjected to persistent philosophical and ethical criticism. Self-avowed "humanists" have attacked Skinner's reduction of human beings to something less than human. Joseph Wood Krutch, in _The Measure of Man,_ was an early critic. He compares _Walden Two_ with earlier Utopias. "Is it not meaningful to say that whereas Plato's Republic and More's Utopia are noble absurdities, *Walden Two* is an ignoble one; that the first two ask men to be more than human, while the second urges them to be less?"[16] Krutch warns that:

> "...if 'adjustment' is not to become 'control' and
> 'conditioning' is to stop short of 'brainwashing,'
> some limits must be set which are not defined or even
> hinted at in such statements as those made by some
> psychologists."[17]

Krutch bears down on Skinner's belief in survival as the highest moral good.

> "Once criticism of Mr. Skinner's first principles
> has been insisted on, it becomes obvious enough
> that 'survival' and 'health' are not actually ends
> at all, but only means. Unless one survives _for_
> something, neither survival nor health has any value
> in itself. But the answer to the question of what
> things are worth living for is not self-evident and
> thus the attempt to avoid value judgments leads back
> around the same circle to which every attempt to make
> a science do something of which it is incapable
> inevitably leads."[18]

Like Skinner, Krutch wants to warn us about threats to our society. But he sees far greater peril in a society programmed by a psychological elite.

> "As influence, power, and authority in our society
> pass, as they are passing, from philosophers and
> theologians into the hands of those who call
> themselves 'human engineers' whether they happen
> to be functioning as lawmakers, publicists, teachers,
> psychologists, or even advertising managers, it is
> passing from those who were at least aware of
> what value judgments they were making to those who are
> not; passing into the hands of men who act on very
> inclusive and fateful judgments while believing they
> are acting on self evident principles immune to criticism.
> Moreover, in so far as their attempt to 'condition'
> the human beings on whom they practice their techniques
> are successful, they make it less and less probable
> that their fateful assumptions will ever be questioned."[19]

Skinner replied to this kind of critcism as follows:

> "One would scarcely guess that the authors [of those
> criticisms of *Walden Two*] are talking about a world

in which there is food, clothing, and shelter for all,
where everyone chooses his own work and works on the
average only four hours a day, where music and the
arts flourish, where personal relationships develop
under the most favorable circumstances, where
education prepares every child for the social and
intellectual life which lies before him, where--in
short--people are truly happy, secure, productive,
creative, and forward looking. What is wrong with
it? Only one thing: someone 'planned it that way.'
If these critics had come upon a society in some
remote corner of the world which boasted similar
advantages, they would have undoubtedly had hailed
it as providing a pattern we all might well follow -
provided that it was clearly the apt result of a
natural process of culture evolution."20

What Skinner does not appear to understand is that the human need for
truly free individual choice is not negotiable, even if it could be
demonstrated, that a culturally harmonious community could be devised
by behavioral technology in which all other human needs are readily
met.

Another well known critic of Skinner's ethical vision is Arthur
Koestler, the novelist, essayist, and philosopher. In *The Ghost in
the Machine*, Koestler attacks behaviorism as a way of understanding
the human species. Koestler argues that behaviorism represents an
inadequately founded science of human behavior.

"...it [behaviorism] has replaced the anthropomorphic
fallacy - ascribing to animals human faculties and
sentiments - with the opposite fallacy denying man
faculties not found in the lower animal; it has sub-
stituted for the erstwhile anthropomorphic view the
view of the rat, a ratomorphic view of man."21

Koestler is arguing for a hierarchical classification of living
beings, in which causal determinism may explain most behavior at lower
levels in the classification, but in which causality becomes less
adequate at the human or upper end of the scale. Thus his most
fundamental criticism of behaviorism:

"Regardless of the verbal acrobatics of Behaviorists
and their allies, the fundamental problem of mind and
matter, of free will versus determinism are still
very much with us, and have acquired a new urgency -
not as a subject of philosophical debate, but because
of their direct bearing on political ethics and
private morals, on criminal justice, psychiatry, and
our whole outlook on life. By the very act of denying

97

the existence of the ghost in the machine - of
mind dependent on, but also responsible for the
actions of the body - we incur the risk of turning
into a very nasty, malevolent ghost."[22]

Another criticism of Skinner's ethical vision focuses on the
connection between values and the ultimate norm of survival. Peter G.
Stalman notes that "...for Skinner, there are not (nor ought there
be) any transcendent social norms against, for instance, murder; all
values are determined relativistically, by what is positively reinforcing to the individual in his particular environment."[23] Since
Skinner has adopted this reinforcement definition of values, that is,
values are whatever may be positively reinforcing to the person or
culture, Stalman argues:

"That he [Skinner] cannot connect values to survival
should have been apparent to Skinner as soon as he
defined values subjectively, in terms of reinforcement,
for then they cannot be consistently or necessarily
related to anything other than those subjective responses
(of individuals or culture); they cannot, for instance,
be linked to survival."[24]

What Stalman and others are attempting to show is that Skinner
has insufficiently accounted for the facts which even he has observed,
namely, that people will choose what is immediately reinforcing while
at the same time acting in ways that ultimately work against the
survival of their culture. Skinner is trying to persuade them not
to do that, to work instead for cultural survival. But that requires
convincing people that their own best interests are to be served not
in immediate gratification, but in deferred gratifications, indeed,
deferred for so long that one generation may not live long enough
to get any immediate rewards. Thus we come to a clash of reinforcers,
weak reinforcers which are vital to survival, in conflict with strong
reinforcers, which are destroying the culture. Skinner is distinguishing, then, between values and the ultimate good. Values are
what people want and try to get; survival is the transcendent good
which people ought to recognize and work to attain.

Another criticism of survival as the ultimate moral norm is
offered by Patrick Bateson: "The survival explanation is necessarily
post hoc, and Skinner is quite unable to state in advance when
cultures should be highly specialized and conformist and when cultures
should be diversified and heterodox."[25] Bateson is pointing out
that Skinner and other social evolutionists who make survival the
ultimate moral norm for a culture are committing the fallacy of
employing an interpretive framework useful for understanding the
past history of a species or a culture, as a source of prescriptions
for what one must do in the future in order to guarantee the survival

of species or of culture. Skinner would argue that behavioral
science is now that precise. But not many other behavioral scientists
would agree with that judgment, and other critics would argue that
the very character of the subject matter, human behavior and human
history, simply cannot be conformed to such an analysis.

Another criticism of Skinner's ethical vision focuses on
another kind of extrapolation. Herbert McClosky says:

> "...I begin to take issue with behaviorists such as
> Skinner when they seek to apply their limited, rudi-
> mentary, (and still poorly-understood) tools to large-
> scale, complex forms of social organizations, including
> (in Skinner's case) entire societies. ...I see little
> ground for believing in either the efficacy or desir-
> ability of systematically applying operant principles
> to large-scale, pluralistic, complex, industrial
> societies."[26]

McClosky not only thinks it is illegitimate to extrapolate from the
laboratory to a large and complex society, he also questions the
means which would be required in to do something like that:

> "...we have reason to doubt that the total or near
> total control required for effective, predictable
> behavior modification on a large scale can be
> achieved without totalitarian and highly authori-
> tarian political systems that most of us would find
> repugnant."[27]

Another critique of Skinner's moral vision is offered by Philip
H. Scribner,[28] using the distinction between "hard determinists" and
"soft determinists." Skinner, of course, is a "hard determinist,"
since he argues that we must believe and act as if every event is
determined by its genetic and conditioning history. Scribner wants
to affirm the general truth of behaviorism, but in a way which allows
for human responsibility and decision making. A "soft determinist"
needs to distinguish between cases of substantial or nearly complete
external compulsion to cases where greater responsibility is
exercised. Scribner believes that there is a kind of soft determinism which can describe the kind of conditioning which will produce
truly free or autonomous human beings. Scribner says that a person
can work toward self-direction by cognitive processes, moral reflection, and evaluation, and thus avoid the spectre of the "automatically
good" person which is described in *Walden Two*. Scribner argues that
a free, self-directed person is much more likely to survive than the
naturally happy members of a controlled society.

Willard Gaylin has summarized the qualities of the good society which Skinner wants:

"It must: (1) provide for order and security; (2) produce necessary goods; (3) maintain a healthy environment; (4) provide for education. All of these vague and general platitudes can exist in a monstrous as well as a benevolent society - depending on who defines 'healthy' or 'necessary', for example. But then he adds two more. He tells us that a good society must: 'Provide for the pursuit and achievement of happiness.' ...but what kind of word is 'happiness,' ...? What kind of behavior is it? How does he measure it? How can he recognize the contingencies for it?"[29]

After examining Skinner's list of the problems which indicate that our society is headed toward self-destruction, Gaylin describes Skinner's Utopia as follows:

"Dr. Skinner is designing the world that he would like now, ...the examples he uses are not even what people in his world like, only what people of his generation like, and that is a world that is being passed by. ...we are asked to do conditioning, starting with the neonate, in order to guarantee the adult behavior in some unknown culture twenty to thirty years later that will not be inhabited by the designer. This time gap also discredits Dr. Skinner's reassurance that the democratic process will be maintained because the principle of making the controller a member of the group he controls should apply to the designer of the culture."[30]

Gaylin asks whether we are at such a desperate point that we need a controlled society to rescue civilization. Gaylin thinks the chances for human survival are good.

"...biologically we can make a better case for man as the loving animal. No species is helpless and dependent for so large a proportion of its life-span as man. Incapable of either fight or flight, the two conventional mechanisms of survival, the defenseless and passive infant survives only in dependency. His very existence depends on the strength and support of the loving adult who will sacrifice himself, if need be, for the survival of the young. It is inconceivable that any species so designed could have survived if this were left to the chance institutions of education and culture. One must assume that built genetically into the organism is a protective response to the helpless member of the species."[31]

In the criticisms cited above and in other literature critizing Skinner, certain themes emerge: (1) Skinner is criticized for reducing human beings to reflexes, stimulus-response causality, and histories of genetic design and reinforcement. This reduction of what it means to be human to complexes of environmentally determined responses has the effect of making human beings no more than very sophisticated and complicated machines, which we shall one day be able to understand, predict and thus control on the basis of the laws governing the behavior of such complex machines. (2) Skinner's view leaves no room for human consciousness, for the mind, for the will, for freedom, for choice, for some inner agency or direction or autonomy. (3) Skinner's vision encourages the use of inhumane forms of treatment, social organization, planning, and control, resulting in totally managed institutions and social orders, with the attending evils of fascism, brain-washing, torture and tyranny. There is no protection, these critics argue, from the evil purposes of evil controllers. And there is no guarantee that scientifically guided controllers will act for the good of the whole society rather than for their own private gains.

This moral debate between Skinner and his critics has gone on for years. In considering the ethics of behavior modification, we need to know about this debate and the issues which are at stake. This is a debate over fundamental ethical goals.

But it is surely not the only arena in which moral discourse about behavior modification needs to occur. This continuing debate between Skinner and his critics has unfortunately diverted attention from ethical questions regarding the application of behavior modification which are more urgently upon us. While Skinner and his critics have been exchanging charge and counter-charge in print and on television, behavior modification methods continue to be developed and applied in a variety of therapeutic settings, in schools, and in institutions for the treatment of mental illness, mental retardation and criminal behavior. Key ethical questions are being faced and decisions are being made every day regarding such uses of behavior modification. But Skinner and his utopian ideas seem to get all of the attention. While applied behaviorism owes a great deal to the research and theories of B. F. Skinner, the most important decisions about the ethics of behavior modification will probably be made far from the field of battle between Skinner and his critics.

D. OTHER BEHAVIORISTS AS ETHICISTS

While the Skinner debate has monopolized public attention, there is a rapidly growing body of literature about applied behaviorism written by psychologists engaged in research and treatment. Many of these psychologists have discussed ethical issues in research and treatment. In this section, we will look at some examples of their thinking.

First we will examine viewpoints in which ethical questions are either treated lightly or in which the ethics of behavior modification are viewed as no different from decisions about other procedures. Then we shall look at viewpoints which hold that there are both similarities between the ethics of behavior modification and other treatments, but that behavior modification methods also raise new ethical questions. Then we shall examine the views of philosophers and theologians.

1. *"The Same in Principle"*:

William R. Morrow and Harvey L. Gochros offer a clear example of the first kind of ethical viewpoint. "We believe that there are ethical problems in the use of behavior-modification techniques, but that these are the same ethical problems that apply to the use of any professional change-agent technique."[32]

Ann B. Smith asks whether there is a conflict between humanism and behavior modification in an article in *The Elementary School Journal*, and concludes that:

> "...behavior modification, if used humanistically, can ... be an effective tool for greater freedom, self expression, and realization of potential. If teachers reject a useful set of principles and methods because of humanistic scruples, the lives of many children may be impoverished. ... there need be no conflict between behavior modification and humanism."[33]

D. A. Begelman takes Smith's point a step further when he says: "... it is possible to argue that the outstanding contribution of the behavioral approach is not technological but moral innovation!" He continues by saying:

"Behaviorists hold that the environmental contingencies responsible for deviant behavior are lawfully related to the latter. The laws in question are considered to be identical in form to those controlling normal behavior."[34] While Begelman does not discount

102

ethical questions in the use of behavior modification, he is suggesting that there may also be important ethical gains from its use because it assumes that the laws of learned behavior are exactly the same for persons who are labeled normal and for persons who are labeled deviant or sick.

Elizabeth Hall has written a very readable and engaging book about the applications of behavior modification. It is entitled *From Pigeons to People*. Toward the end of her book, she asks about the potentially ethically desirable and undesirable effects of behavior modification.

"Behavior Shapers themselves believe that if their principles are adopted in prisons, hospitals, schools, businesses and the home, crime will decrease, children will learn more, employees will be happier, businesses will make more money and life will be more pleasant.

"Used properly bemod (sic) can do some of these things all of the time and all of these things some of the time. The big problem is to see that it is used properly."[35]

Hall says that the key to a "proper" use of behavior modification is to be found in the kind of society where it is used:

"The battle over bemod really boils down to three related questions: who is going to control the behavior? Why is it being controlled? Does the control limit a person's freedom? Behavior modification in a dictatorship is dangerous. There is no argument on this point. In a democratic society, however, the controllers are teachers, parents, therapists and employers. Students, children, patients and workers remain free to counter control."[36]

In reply to questions about the loss of freedom and moral choice, Hall says:

"... some philosophers are uncomfortable because they see behavior modification leading to a world of moral robots. They want man free to choose between good and evil....

"Praise and reward, combined with mild, pain-free punishment, is not likely to lead to the abuses that philosophers fear. Used properly, bemod could help us to reach a world in which individuals wished and worked to be responsible and sensitive citizens.

"Perhaps the answer to the problem posed by behavior
modification is not suppression but education.
Knowledge is power. The more people know about the
promises and possible abuses of behavior shaping,
the less any of us have to worry about the world
of the clockwork orange."[37]

These are reassuring words, but they do not really illumine the
ethical questions which must be faced. Hall is assuming that in the
democratic society, teachers, parents, therapists, and employers will
be working for the common good, and that children, patients and workers
will have the freedom and power to prevent abuses of behavior modification. She is also attributing exclusively positive moral value to
education or information, which it surely does not merit. So while
we must agree with her that behavior modification should be properly
rather than improperly used, we also need to confront the possibility
that the power of behavior modification can be abused, even in a
democratic society.

Herbert Keleman has taken up ethical questions raised by behavior
modification, and, like Begelman, suggests that a positive ethical
gain can come from behavior modification.

"The extent to which the influence attempt - despite
its manipulative component - allows for or even
enhances the person's freedom of choice, the extent
to which the relationship between influencer and
influencee is reciprocal, the extent to which the
situation is oriented toward the welfare of the
influencee rather than the welfare of the influencing
agent - all of these are of great moment from an
ethical point of view."[38]

Keleman urges behavior modifiers to work in three specific ways
toward positive ethical outcomes: an increased public awareness of
the processes of manipulation; building resistance to manipulation
into the process itself; and setting the enhancement of freedom of
choice as a positive goal for behavior modification. Keleman is
also aware of the possibilities for abuse and he notes with some
concern that social science is increasingly used by the government,
by military organizations, by welfare institutions and the like.

So far we have looked at some examples of ethical thinking which
acknowledge that ethical problems arise in the use of behavior modification, but which argue that there are also positive ethical outcomes,
indeed, results only made possible through applied behavior modification.

2. "Similarities but New Questions Too"

We now turn to examples of ethical analysis showing greater awareness by behaviorists of the complex and subtle ethical issues which are involved in the use of behavior modification.

Leonard Krasner has published two extended discussions of the ethics of behavior modification. In the earlier essay, he begins by arguing that "... behavioral scientists are still hiding between a set of myths, hiding from the large issue which places them today - that of the ethical implications of the controlability of human behavior."[39] Krasner identifies these myths as the belief that the therapist is not responsible for changes which take place in their patients, the myth of mental illness, and the myth of 'robotism,' that is, the belief that discovering the power of environmental control, human beings have been reduced to robots. Krasner states his own behavioral credo:

> "I would conceive of man clearly in the robot end of
> the continuum. That is, his behavior can be completely
> determined by outside stimuli. Even if man's behavior
> is determined by internal mediating events..., these
> events can be manipulated by outside stimuli so that
> it is these stimuli which basically determine our
> behavior."[40]

But Krasner does not leave it there, with mechanistic determinism. He argues that human beings can and should behave as if they were actually free and able to have some control over their own destiny. "Thus to the extent that man can believe in terms of having alternative behaviors available, to that extent they are free."[41]

Krasner goes on to emphasize mutual responsibility in the relationship between the therapist and the patient. "A major implication of the behavioral viewpoint is to increase the responsibility of both therapist and patient, to get them both out from behind the myth that we are not responsible human beings."[42]

Krasner turns out to be very concerned about our culture's drift from freedom to control. He puts it this way:

> "I am deeply concerned that while we worry about the
> problems of existence, being, becoming, and growing,
> the knowledge, information and techniques of controlling
> behavior will be established in the real world outside,
> and our freedom, however defined, will be gone; and,
> as the crowning blow, we will not be aware of it and
> we will still think of ourselves as free to exist,
> to be, to become, to grow, and to self-actualize."[43]

Krasner seems to be distinguishing between two senses of freedom. One sense of freedom is that feeling of choice among behaviors which we can have if we acknowledge the extent to which behavior is environmentally determined, and if we make the kinds of choices which will increase mutual responsibility and accountability for arranging desirable environmental reinforcers. The other sense of freedom is the dream-like myth with which we can reassure ourselves while not realizing that freedom is being taken from us. Krasner is facing here the same logical and moral dilemmas confronted by Skinner.

In the more recent essay, Krasner takes up ethical questions about behavior modification in discussing the formation of values in the training of psychologists. He begins by observing that behavior modification is not unlike other attempts to influence persons

> "... it seems that traditional psychotherapy can be interpreted as individuals of middle class background (the therapists), who persuade other individuals of similar background to adopt their way of looking at life. To the extent that this persuasion or influence is successful, the patient will be considered improved."[44]

Krasner then reflects upon the choices which therapists must make:

> "In whatever setting he may be, the behavior modifier arrives at choice points in his procedure. These involve a decision on what behaviors to shape, modify, or reinforce. The modifier must consider who will benefit from the consequences of this particular change in behavior, the individual or society. In most instances, both will equally benefit and this can be expressed by saying that the individual is able to minimize the reinforcement possibilities from his environment (society). However, there are instances in which there is a clear conflict."[45]

What should the therapist do when there is such a conflict?

> "... I will not try to avoid this issue and will take a stand that the therapist is always society's agent."[46]

Krasner does not mean to say that the effect of behavior modification is always or simply adjustment or adaptation of a deviant individual to the dominant society. He argues that the therapist as society's agent "helps change individual behavior and also social institutions themselves."[47]

In these two essays by Krasner, we discover a more penetrating ethical sensitivity and a more adequate analysis than we found in the previous examples. The argument goes something like this: because behaviors are environmentally caused in increasingly knowable and predictable ways, and because in behavior modification we are working with a learning model and not an illness or deviance model, we need to find ways to maximize clear gains in responsibility for both the therapists and the patient. The therapist does carry a heavy degree of responsibility because the therapist arranges for environmental contingencies to shape and direct desirable behaviors. And while the therapist is primarily the agent of a client and while usually the goals of the client and the goals of society are in harmony, there are cases where conflict exists. In those cases, the therapist must be primarily an agent of society.

Albert Bandura holds a viewpoint much like Krasner's. He stresses the ways in which other forms of psychotherapy try to control attitudes and values covertly, while behavior modification openly tries to control only behavior. Where there are conflicts between the client's goals and society's goals, Bandura advocates the promotion of freedom of choice tempered by a sense of social obligation.[48]

Like Krasner, Bandura is aware that the client and society may demand incompatible aims. But unlike Krasner, Bandura is not so sure that the therapist is primarily an agent of society. Bandura classifies such conflict - cases under three headings: In cases of correcting self-restraints, where the client wishes to change destructive behaviors in his or her own situations, any objectives are morally permissible except those which would make the clients socially irresponsible. In cases of behavioral defects, where the client needs to acquire new behaviors, the ethically proper therapeutic goal is to increase self-determination. In cases where society imposes changed behavior on a possibly unwilling person or group, Bandura argues for a careful ethical analysis, which must always include the possibility that the therapist may support socially disapproved choices, for the sake of what the therapist judges to be the best overall interests of the client.[49]

Leonard P. Ullmann proposes to address ethical questions in behavior therapy by considering the analogy between the behavioral therapist and leaders of social movements. Because behavior therapy works out of a learning model rather than an illness model, Ullmann suggests that abnormal behavior and social movements share similar problems of definition, target behaviors, and techniques. In his analysis of social psychology and its theories of social movements, Ullmann notes that social movements are distinguished in three ways: they are statistically different from the main society which they are a part. They are characterized by generalized feelings of being unhappy or upset with present conditions. And there is clear non-conformity with aspects of the dominant culture. Ullmann says, "... it will be argued that abnormal behavior involves designation to a group and that the therapist acts as a leader who encourages membership in some groups and defection from others."[50] Ullmann describes the relationship between deviant social movements and the larger culture:

> "... changes in values, norms, and social organizations are necessary for the continued survival of the society. If the dominant majority in the society does not make necessary adjustments, then social movements, even if they are at first repressed and particularly if they are in harmony with the broader values of the society, may well be the saviors of the society."[51]

Moving then to a discussion of the ethical responsibility of the behavioral therapist, Ullmann rejects the explanation which attributes failure of therapy to the choices of the client.

> "If the therapist believed in freedom of choice, he could solve this problem. ... he cannot believe in freedom of choice and his very competence as a therapist increases his responsibility.... For this reason, it seems wrong to say that anything a client requests is ethically acceptable. In short, when therapist A deals with patient B, he must think of the consequences for person C."[52]

Ullmann takes note of the ethical problems involved when control groups are used in research or environmental conditions are manipulated to influence people without their consent. These procedures suggest

> "... that one group of people knows better than another what is good for it. By implication these are conditions in which people may be exploited and influenced without prior consent. These people have not broken any explicit legislated rule and their behavior is not formulated as sick."[53]

Ullmann concludes that:

> "... by following the analogy of the social movement, the ethical limits of behavior therapy may be charted. By reference to the corpus of theoretical, judicial, and social experience developed for social movements, the behavior therapist's enterprise may be legitimized without recourse to a medical model."[54]

That means that "the limitations imposed on the behavior therapist are essentially the limitations imposed on the citizen in general: not to violate the rules that make social living possible.

"... if the behavior therapist is a leader, where shall he lead? Within the limits presented, the behavior therapist evaluates and represents the realities of the social environment.... The behavior therapist as a leader encourages defection from some movements and sub- scription to others. The range of behavior encouraged by social movements and the social utility of such move- ments argues against the notion that the present formulation must lead to automaton conformity.... The model of social movements permits the behavior therapist to serve both the individual and society without violating his trust to either, and without seeking his source of legitimacy from the medical model or by denying his responsibility."[55]

Ullman's effort to illumine the ethical questions facing the behavior therapist by reference to leaders of social movements does not prove to be as fruitful at the end as we might have hoped. While it is helpful to search for some alternative to the medical model of sickness or deviance, it appears that Ullmann has taken recourse to a theory of the socially functional character of social movements and their leaders, with the result that a kind of social-science-based natural harmony theory emerges, in which the truly difficult ethical dilemmas are no longer taken with full seriousness. Like Krasner and Bandura, Ullmann acknowledges the dilemmas of power and respon- sibility which are faced by the therapist, and like Krasner he locates the primary foundation of values in the society which the therapist serves.

However creatively this message of adaptation is stated, it is still not helpful ethically. Aside from the immense difficulties in trying to state what are the root values of the dominant society, this formula is deficient because it attempts to derive the "ought" from the "is."

Margaret Lloyd, in discussing the possibility of licensing for applied behavior modification or behavioral therapists, made the following observation about one of the ethical problems being faced:

"... society seems temporarily at a loss about how to handle misuse which occurs in conjunction with changing or restructuring environments. This is especially true when the individuals involved in the restructuring are not participating voluntarily, such as behavior modifi- cation programs in prisons, mental hospitals, and hos- pitals for the retarded.... The fact is that most state

licensing procedures affect only those therapists in
private practice and therefore exclude from control
those very people working in the areas where the
problems are most acute."[56]

Another approach to the ethical use of behavior modification is
advocated by Jon E. Krapfl. He employs Skinner's notion of counter-
control and tries to define it in more practical terms:

"There are several ways in which we might contribute
to the development of these counter controlling practices:
One, train the public in the use of behavior principles
and practices. No man can be more free than the one
who knows the variables of which his behavior is a
function... Two, support and design mechanisms for
public review of efforts and effects. This model
basically entails advance review of proposed practices
and post hoc analysis of effectiveness by a body representative of the general public.... Three, a final
step would be to train the reviewers so that they could
make disinterested, objective, but worthwhile evaluations
of behavioral programs."[57]

Stephanie B. Stolz cites research on ethical questions which
were raised by review committees at the National Institute of Mental
Health, as these committees considered grant applications in the area
of behavior modification.

"At first glance, the ethics of therapy appear clear
and straight forward: Therapy should provide the
maximum benefit to the patient and to the society,
with careful consideration and resolution of conflicts
when they occur.... However, the high proportion of
therapy applications where reviewers felt there were
ethical problems is testimony to the fact that such
considerations and balances are easier to state in the
abstract than to observe in practice."[58]

Stolz goes on to list some of the areas in which ethical questions
were most frequently raised: Who is responsible for defining deviance?
What are the justifications for the intervention? Have informed consent procedures been carefully employed? Have unjustified risks been
taken? And have aversive therapy procedures been used? Stolz stated
that the review committees were always careful to inquire whether the
risks involved in some of these instances could be definitively demonstrated to be outweighed by the benefits to the subjects, not the
benefits to the researchers or therapists.

These observations from Lloyd, Krapfl and Stolz suggest that
persons who are engaged in professional practice and those who monitor

professional practice are aware of the delicate moral questions involved in applied behavior modification, and are less likely to be
caught up in the rarefied atmosphere of the Skinner debate.

Robert Neville has discussed some of the ethical and philosophical
issues of behavior control in a paper given at the annual meeting of
the American Association for the Advancement of Science in 1972.
One central issue is the definition of health.

"I suspect the real meaning of the notion of health,
operating in our every day judgments dealing with
mental health, has to do with maximizing our various
capacities of response, in some compatible harmony
with each other, so as to be able to take advantage
of the variable environment. ... if this is near to
the meaning of 'health,' the criteria, in fact,
vary with variations in the environment providing
opportunities for human response. ... because the
important variations in the human environment are
often cultural ones, personal health is extraordi-
narily relative to cultural differences and differences
in life situations."[59]

But health also has public as well as cultural dimensions.

"Health defines a person's functioning with respect to
his physical and social environment from a public point
of view. It conceives his behavior from the standpoint
of being observable by another, even if the observation
is only through self-revelatory discussion. Health
necessarily is defined this way if public judgments are
to be made about it and professionals are to help in its
development and maintenance.

"But people also have private sides, difficult to define,
but acknowledged in many ways. People have private
reasons for putting other things above health sometimes.
... if our society had not decided to respect peoples'
private choices about health, there would be compulsory
health management, including universal, socially defined
education. And there would be no question about the
morality of behavior control, only about its efficiency.
But one of the reasons B. F. Skinner's writings make so
many people uneasy is that he defines people only publicly,
reduces happiness to health, and allows privacy to be
prized only when it makes no difference."[60]

Neville argues that this right of choice is particularly important in considering the use of behavior control mechanisms, because

of the sensitive care which is required to make sure that informed
consent is secured. Neville argues the importance of securing consent even for the criminal:

"A criminal is sentenced to prison in the alleged
interest of society. If we put aside for the moment
cases where imprisonment amounts to protective custody,
nobody would pretend incarceration is in the interest
of the prisoner except accidentally. So far as I understand our penal system, furthermore, the social interest
in incarceration includes motives of punishment, or
protecting society, and of rehabilitation, ordered with
respect to each other by rules of self-deception and
hyprocrisy.

"Now suppose, if my hypothesis not so far fetched, that
behavior control techniques can be developed that would
punish the criminal, protect the society from his
future depredations, and rehabilitate him, all more
effectively and with less cost to the society than
incarceration. What is to keep us from adopting them
immediately?

"I think we should hesitate out of respect for the
criminal's integrity. ... I cannot think of any
social purposes justifying dehumanization that would
not be more efficiently accomplished by simply killing
the criminal."[61]

James G. Holland, in a symposium sponsored by the National
Institute of Mental Health, discussed some of the ethical dimensions
of applied behavior modification.

"Behavior modification shares with other therapies
all of the usual ethical problems of informed consent,
privileged communications, etc. But behavior modification procedures add new problems. The new ethical
considerations arise from the very strength of the
technique as administered or promised in the near
future."[62]

Holland is concerned about monitoring behavior modification in
the absence of clearly defined professional societies and ethics.
"... responsibility for its use does not rest solely with a small
identifiable professional group guided by an ethical code and easily
held accountable by society..."[63] Holland refers here to applications of behavior modification which occur in institutional settings,
where the persons primarily responsible for charting behaviors and
distributing reinforcers may not be professional psychologists, but

are likely to be parents, teachers, guards, orderlies, or other persons who have understandable personal reasons for wanting compliant behavior, but may lack the kind of training needed to carry out the task professionally.

Holland is most concerned about the possibility that behavior modification techniques will be employed by those who currently hold power in a given social system, and who can be expected to use it for their own ends.

"The work of the psychologists, like that of any other scientist, is channelled by a contingency management system in the service of the goals of our present political organization and corporate-guided society. Our science is not neutral; it is used for the selfish ends of our society.... The use of the growing technology of contingency management is likely to further the interest of the few at the expense of the many."[64]

Holland calls upon psychologists to prevent this abuse. "The behavioral psychologist is preparing procedures which past and present facts indicate will be used by those in positions of power for their ends rather than for the objective of the individual whose behavior is being manipulated. In an effort to curtail their use, the psychologist must do research which will permit countercontrol by individuals or groups lacking resources."[65]

Once again the discussion has come to questions of who has power, how power should be used, and how such power can be more fairly distributed, so that it is not used by the powerful at the expense of the powerless.

I. J. Barrish has attempted to reply to some of the objections to applied behavior modification. In discussing the objection that the behavior modifier, not the client, determines goals and techniques, Barrish says "...the selection of goals in therapy or how the client should act in the future ...is a moral not a scientific decision. This decision is made implicitly or explicitly in most treatment situations."[66]

In dealing with the objection that behavior modification invades privacy or is conducted without the consent of the subject, Barrish argues that the specificity inherent in behavior modification works to protect privacy and consent.

"This necessity for specificity virtually guarantees that the client will be aware of any modifications to be made. In addition, since most modification techniques involve the cooperation of the client, another safeguard is provided."[67]

Barrish does acknowledge that it is very important to specify precisely the procedures which will be used in obtaining the consent of the client "because consent is a behavior and it can be manipulated through the use of contingencies of reward... or punishment...."[68]

Barrish also asks about the conflict between personal rights and social standards. "... the rationale being used to force treatment on the patient clearly emanates from the patient's role as a burden on the society when it is conceivable that the patient had no power in determining that very role."[69] But it is very difficult to tell whether a given patient has chosen that role of sick person or has been socially assigned to that role. People may begin careers as "mental patients" simply because they are initially irritating or offensive to those about them. (Goffman, Szasz) Or they may begin by experiencing frightening schizophrenic episodes which may be aimed at reintegration (Boisen, Laing), but which are treated as sicknesses requiring incarceration and involuntary treatment. We cannot justify involuntary behavior modification for such persons simply because they are now "burdens on society." Continued involuntary treatment may simply confirm that status, rather than appealing to their own remaining resources for healthy decision-making.

Perry London provides a sensitive and helpful analysis of ethical aspects of behavior modification. He begins by issuing this challenge:

"The enormous risks involved make it urgent for intelligent people of good will, especially the scientists and technologists who are most responsible for inventing and testing the techniques of control, to plan, carefully and considerately, how to do their work with the least threat to human freedom and the most promise of promoting mankind's welfare."[70]

London does not give pat reassurance like those who say that behavior modification is still so undeveloped as to merit little concern.

"There is probably little point today, if there ever was one, in debating at length whether or not behavior-control technology is feasible or should generally be attempted or avoided. In general, no such choice is any longer possible. What remains is to determine the characteristics of this technology, the rules of implementing controls, and the purposes which it should serve."[71]

London agrees with other behaviorists that there has always been mutual influence or control exercised in human affairs. But he stresses the important difference that behavioral technology makes:

"True technology is not only deliberate but precise. It demands four capacities: (1) to produce a specific variety of effects, (2) to control the intensity of effects, (3) to specify the domain of effects, and (4) to control the duration of effects. With respect to behavior, none of these capabilities has really been within our grasp until very recently, and it will still be a long time, maybe eternally long until they are eternally so."[72]

London makes these predictions about future forms of behavior control:

"In general, information controls, and some drugs, will have their main impact on individual mores and morals, fostering self-preoccupation, and their social consequences will come for the waves made in the multitudes of individual lives. On the other hand, coercive controls, such as brain implants, will have their greatest impact from the top levels of society, stimulating political, ethical, and philosophical controversy as they emerge and undermining moral traditions by fostering scepticism about the assumptions on which those traditions are based."[73]

London states that it is not just behavioral technology, but our addiction to technology in general which is capable of changing our attitudes towards moral decisions. "By fostering routines which smooth living, general technology tends to undermine the exercise of moral sensibilities; it reduces the number of conscious and deliberate choices needing to be made, which tends to lull us into accepting whatever we are used to, good or bad."[74]

London discussed the use of behavioral technology in politics and economics.

"The most important practical constraints on the widespread use of coercive behavior controls are economic, not ethical or scientific ones. For most political purposes, which is where pervasive control appears most threatening at first blush, it is probably not needed in any refined form. The harsh reality of political manipulation and its bloody corollary, military force, is that man is already the fanciest conceivable machinery widely available in huge lots at pathetically low cost and docile (educable) enough for most purposes, that with relatively little maintenance cost, he can be gotten voluntarily just about anything. Under the circumstances, no one is

likely to go about scrambling peoples brains just
because he has the means for doing so."[75]

With technology having so much influence, London argues that
it is important that scientists, engineers, and technicians should
be in dialogue with political philosophers, theologians, and social
theorists in order to develop better ethical guidelines. Without
such guidelines,

"... the ethical applications of behavior control will
incorporate the views of human nature implied by it.
Those views are borrowed from the scientific beliefs
that made the experiments that found the results that
built the technology in the first place. So the under-
pinnings of the ethical system are fastened to a scientific
model of man."[76]

which is to say, a machine model.

London speaks of the root conflict between a scientific and
humanistic model.

"... humanism is rooted inextricably in a moral system
which is threatened by the machine model of man, and
which would demand political or religious opposition
to that model even if it were 'true' and even if it
were evident that the humanist argument is mounted on
errors of observation, which assumed that the appearance
of uniqueness is uniqueness, or an error of logic,
which neglects the possibility that hard machines may
feel like people but don't say so."[77]

London focuses his analysis of the ethical use of behavior control in this way: "The moral problem of behavior control is the
problem of how to use power justly. This is no new question, but
critical questions in human experience rarely are."[78] London states
that:

"The problem of how to plan the general control of
power over people applies to the control of behavioral technology as well. Until its dangers
are apparent, there is no just way to legislate its
use; as the dangers grow visible, tentative strategies for controlling them can be conceived and
executed when the need is clear - but not before.
It would pervert justice to suppress in her name
evils that are only hypothetical."[79]

London argues that while the just distribution of power is an old question, behavioral technology puts the old questions in an entirely new light, because of the vastly increased power of the behavioral methods available. He proposes dealing with these new difficulties as follows:

"The danger is that even its most benevolent use
runs the risk of eroding freedom when it takes place
by the decision of anyone other than the person on
whom it is used. And in a free but complex society,
that decision must sometimes be made by other people,
and even against the subject's wishes. The ethical
challenge emphasized by behavior technology is that
of how to preserve or enhance individual liberty
under circumstances where its suppression will frequently be justified not only by the common welfare
but for the individual's happiness."[80]

London says we can no longer use the notion of individual consent or will as a criterion for liberty.

"As long as it was true historically that there was
no sure way to enslave people except 'against their
will,' individual consent or will was a reasonable
criterion for liberty. Once will itself can be
readily manipulated, though, it stops being a useful
measure of the limits for exerting power; ... Behavior-
control technology brings no conceptual novelty to
the process; it just makes it easier to maintain
power over others once someone wishes to do so.

"Behavior control means that some people have power
over others; freedom means they do not. The ethical
problems of freedom and control reduce to the conflict
between these simple meanings, no matter how elegant
the technical apparatus of power becomes."[81]

Like other behaviorists whose views we have examined, London says that "in order to defend individual freedom, it is necessary to enhance the power of individuals. If behavior technology endangers freedom by giving refined power to controllers, then the antidote which promotes freedom is to give more refined power over their own behavior to those who are endangered."[82] This proposal is akin to Skinner's idea of countercontrol, although London does not use that term.

Since London has argued that consent or the will are no longer trustworthy safeguards for individual liberty, he proposes "aware-ness" as a satisfactory substitution. "It is awareness, a set of higher processes in the brain with which we recognize ourselves as having a self and from which we derive the special human powers of control which animal passions could not supply.

"Awareness is the conscious processing of information which includes selecting it, storing it, and acting upon it. And the processing of information is the essence of behavior control."[83]

So London advocates a concentration on human awareness, "... on the subjective self, not to the exclusion of its surroundings, but for the expansion of its own contents..."[84] Expanded awareness, London concludes, is the way to increase personal mastery and resist external control.

London summarizes his discussion:

"... what actions do the ethics of awareness demand? There are at least four: of technology, it demands that individual development be maximized and people provided with the instruments of self-control; men must know their tools. Of politics, it demands that men must be free and the machinery of government forever vulnerable to individual actions against it; men must have their rights. Of free men, it demands that they be conscious of the need to share the world with other men and exercise restraint on their own willfulness; men must know some limits. Of society, it demands that it renounce coercion as its chief instrument of control and substitute persuasive means which individuals may finally take or leave, even at some perils to us all; men must take some risks."[85]

Of all of the ethical analyses offered by behaviorists, Perry London's is in my judgment, the best of the lot. But there is one key point in his analysis where I think he falters badly, and that is where he warns that behavioral technology can control or manipulate the consent of the will. He attributes too much power to behavior modification. But then London develops an ethic of "awareness," in which he locates all of the will's functions of reflection and decision-making. As I argued in the previous chapter, reason, or the mind, or thinking, or London's "awareness" are required for a strong, healthy will. But they are no substitute.

Our final example of a behaviorist's proposals for using behavior modification on the ethical use of behavior ethically is provided by Israel Goldiamond, in his essay, "Toward a Constructional Approach to Social Problems." Goldiamond suggests using the Constitution of the United States as a model contract, pointing out that "... the powers assigned to one of the contracting parties,

118

namely, the Federal Government, are limited to those explicitly stated in the contract..."[86] Thus, he argues, the Federal Constitution stands in sharp contrast to the total systems developed in mental hospitals and prisons.

Using Goffman's concept of "total institutions," where the three major areas of life, sleep, play, and work are all governed by the rules of the institution, Goldiamond observes that successful therapy is defined by the disappearance of the problem that got the individual into difficulty in the first place. Goldiamond rejects this definition of health as the absence of problems. In its place, he advocates a "constructional" rather than a pathological orientation, as better meeting the legal and ethical requirements of real treatment. "This is defined as an orientation whose solution to problems is the construction of repertoires (or their reinstatement or transfer to new situations) rather than the elimination of repertoires."[87] (By "repertoires," he means a series of learned patterns of behavior).

Goldiamond recognizes that there are situations in which a pathological orientation must be taken into account, but he wants that paired with a constructional approach, and he argues that this constructional-pathological pairing cuts across and includes all other theoretical models of treatment. "... our aim is not to develop a new therapy which supplants others, but to make explicit what goes on in psychotherapy or treatment, however named."[88] This approach, he argues, can be judged to be in keeping with the Federal Constitution because it includes "... contracting with the patient on outcomes and procedures we both consider worthwhile, rather than considering the patient as a third party who is to meet ends defined by two other parties, using procedures they set."[89]

Translating the implications of this philosophy of treatment into one of the clauses from the Federal Constitution, Goldiamond suggests it would be stated the following way: "Intervention by means of the constructional model discussed in the previous section is limited to constructions of the specific outcomes contracted. All other patterns are reserved to the subjects."[90]

This way of stating treatment philosophy also moves beyond the medical or pathological model.

"What is considered pathology may also be defined as a competent operant, maintained by the environmental reinforcers it produces, but presently (or foreseeably) producing these at high cost or otherwise placing the person in jeopardy. ... the person is thereby regarded as a competent individual, like thee and me, who may

119

have had to resort to unusual tactics to get what
thou and I have obtained through conventional means."[91]

Goldiamond summarizes his proposals:

"The major thrust of my argument is that the practical
system developed along those lines accords with the
Constitutional premise of a government limited to those
powers and explicitly specified (along with those implied
as necessary for such purposes), with all other powers
residing within the people. The system also accords
with related ethical premises. Ends and means are
concorded and, indeed, explicitly so with every step
toward the outcome a faithful miniature of the larger
program. The issue is viewed in a social context in
which definitions of repertoires are social and have
social and individual consequences. Accordingly,
decision processes enter not only into definition of
problems but also of solution. The procedures described
increase the likelihood of obtaining the information
necessary for a rational decision process. The solution
requires construction of additional options for the individual, thereby increasing his freedom. And he is described in terms which enhance his human dignity. These
constitutional and ethical implications derive from the
research requirements of the model, which are also
critical to its social application."[92]

Now that we have completed this examination of examples of
ethical thinking by behaviorists, we need to summarize and evaluate.

First we should note the differences between Skinner and the
others. Skinner offers a utopian moral vision. None of the other
behaviorists we examined are quite so bold. Other behaviorists
deal with issues raised by Skinner such as freedom and countercontrol,
but they are not so preoccupied with the vision of a perfectly controlled human society. On the other hand, many of these other
behaviorists are much more aware of specific ethical questions in
applied behavioral technology - a just distribution of power,
access to power, and the safeguards which are needed with new and
powerful behavior technologies.

Evaluated according to the three elements of ethical thinking
described at the beginning of this chapter, Skinner has a normative
moral vision but neglects principles and procedures of application,
and neglects technical aspects of application. The other behaviorists
surveyed are better at the technical and application questions, but
are weaker in expressing a normative moral vision. Several of them,
especially Krasner, London, and Goldiamond, use the ideals of

American democracy as a guiding moral vision. Goldiamond even uses the Federal Constitution for his principled statement of moral norms. All three are concerned with a just distribution of power. And all of them affirm the importance of freedom and personal liberty.

Though these ethical themes are consistent with beliefs about the human good which lie at the heart of constitutional democracies like the United States, they are not sufficiently developed as a coherent moral vision to provide sure guidance for practical questions of applied behavior modification facing us today. And these themes do not represent a vision of the good which transcends a particular national or cultural set of norms. However a normative moral vision is grounded, it must embrace all humankind.

E. RELIGIOUS AND PHILOSOPHICAL ANALYSES OF BEHAVIORISM

So far, there have not been many efforts to analyze behavior modification ethically from a religious or philosophical standpoint. This neglect was noted and discussed briefly in the first chapter. But there are a few noteworthy examples, to which we now turn.

In an essay which asks the question, "Can a Christian Ethic Condone Behavior Modification?", Ronald G. Alexander advocates at least one form of behavior modification:

"We choose operant conditioning for our focus because it can so readily lend itself in its form to humanitarian purposes, which it certainly has in common with 'Christian' ethics, and because Skinner sees operant conditioning as playing an essential role in his vision of the new society, which also has been a dream of the Christian."[93]

Alexander believes that one can compare Skinner's visionary morality with similar visions of the morally perfect age characterizing Christian thought.

In another unpublished paper, Alexander discusses the importance of moral ideas or ethical values in the contract made between the patient and the therapist. "... it is often the case that the patient seeking help from a therapist does not have a clear idea as to behavioral goals and that the therapist in such a situation cannot help but to bring his own moral ideas into play into conversations with the patient."[94] Alexander argues that moral sensibilities need to be respected on both sides.

"... if the client's goal is at odds with the therapist's moral code, then the therapist has a

right not to be the client's instrument. At the
same time, it has already been established that the
therapist has no right to bully the client into
seeing things his way. After a calm and rational
discussion of the professional problem, the therapist
may see fit to refer the client to another clinician."[95]

Alexander notes the problem with using "society" as the moral
norm, since "... society is composed of groups and units, and these
groups and units can have opposing as well as differing ethical
principles."[96] But this does not mean that the therapist is without
guidelines. Here Alexander cites operant conditioning, as in his previous paper, as a general moral principle.

"However, the behavior modifier is not left without
a starting point in the development of an ethic. He
can turn to the theme and thrust of the major method
of behavior modification, i.e., operant conditioning,
as a paradigm. This paradigm emphasizes positive
reinforcement and plays down aversive consequences...."

"I found operant conditioning a useful starting place
because it has affinitives with ethical principles
clearly recognizable to the general public. It is
commensurate with the Jewish and Christian dictum of
'love your fellowman.' It certainly has an element
of respect lying implicitly behind it."[97]

Alexander does acknowledge that operant conditioning can also be used
for negative or dishonorable purposes, but still maintains that it is
intrinsically good in its emphasis on the positive and its rejection
of the negative.

While it is heartening to see a Christian moral philosopher
discussing the ethics in behavior modification, it is disappointing
that Alexander has not developed his moral case for operant conditioning more fully. He does not deal with the use of power, with
potential abuses, and he has not stated a general set of ethical
principles derived from the Judaic and Christian traditions.

Bernard Häring, the Roman Catholic moral theologian, discusses
the ethics of behavior control in his recent book, *Ethics of Manipulation*. Häring stresses uniquely human characteristics which cannot
be ignored or violated in research or treatment. "Manipulation, as
such, is not a great sin or a sin at all. The evil is in the trans-
gression of the limits posed by human freedom and dignity."[98]

Häring says:

> "It is my thesis that he [man] has to interpret his
> stewardship in the light of his noble vocation. In
> that interpretation, he can freely interfere with
> and manipulate the functions of his <u>bios</u> and <u>psyche</u>
> in so far as this does not degrade him or diminish
> his own or his fellowman's dignity and freedom."[99]

That means, according to Häring,

> "... that we have not only the right and duty to
> explore the dimensions of therapy but can go beyond
> that concept and acknowledge our right to plan a
> change, to pilot evolution, even where our own
> physiological, biological and physiological nature
> is concerned. Under God, man is providence for
> himself. He has a right and duty to plan his future
> in so far as he can know and interpret his situation."[100]

Having stated this promising general principle, Häring launches
into a vigorous attack against B. F. Skinner. "... Skinner seems to
be unable to distinguish between manipulating persons and their minds,
and on the other hand, engaging in genuine, liberating dialogue."[101]
Häring suggests that a Skinnerian world-view espousing environmental
determinism in which people are manipulated by a scientific elite is
a dangerous influence in our midst. "We have to examine our whole
culture and the recent development of predominant ideologies in
order to understand and evaluate such a break with the best of our
past history and humanistic tradition."[102] He goes on to say that
"... behavior management, with no regard for freedom and dignity, is
an alarming sign of the sickness of the great part of our society,
and especially of our higher education."[103]

According to Häring,

> "... for us Christians, a mere therapy of external
> behavior is unthinkable. We do not believe that one
> can make good the fruits without making the tree good....
> We believe in the reality of man's conscience, in the power
> of inner freedom, in the decisive value of inner convic-
> tions, and in a person's capacity to search for ultimate
> meaning, the search for what is truthful and good, and
> to act by the power of inner and freely acquired
> modivations."[104]

Häring does acknowledge a positive contribution:

> "... the behavioral sciences have corrected an erroneous
> concept of unlimited freedom that would allow an imperative

or legalistic morality. And at the same time they have
enabled us to see more clearly concrete possibilities
to improve human conditions, to increase our own freedom,
and to create conditions in which our freedom and that of
our fellowmen can best develop."[105]

He concludes with a cautious word of approval:

"Behavior therapy should make use of the behavioral
sciences, including some of Pavlov's and Skinner's
best insights, but with great discernment. The
final effectiveness and justification of genetic
and environmental therapy lies in a total education
towards freedom in conscience, and a responsible and
generous use of freedom for the common good."[106]

It is unfortunate, after beginning with such a promising effort
to clarify theological and ethical discriminations regarding manipulation, that Häring should turn his entire attention to Skinner's
philosophy of environmental determinism. Because Häring is so
alarmed about Skinner's attacks on freedom and dignity, he does not
really deal at all with practical ethical choices about specific
behavior modification procedures. He does not treat the problem
cases which were analyzed by the behaviorists discussed in the previous
section of this chapter. While we should heed Häring's warnings
about the limits of manipulation, he has not helped us move toward
a more useful ethical principle for the practical problems of applied
behavior modification.

Our final example of an ethical analysis of behavior modification
appears in an essay by Gardner C. Quarton, "Deliberate Efforts to
Control Human Behavior and Modify Personality," which appeared in
Daedalus Magazine in the summer issue, 1967. Quarton begins with a
helpful admonition:

"An emotional reaction to the idea of behavior control
seems to lead to a short-circuiting of the process of
evaluation... In this short-circuited discussion, the
leap from the idea to plans for immediate social action
omits a review of the factual issues that would seem to
be necessary for a more deliberate evaluation. Very often
there is a failure to distinguish between facts and values,
and between values and proposals for social action."[107]

Quarton also reminds us that we become needlessly preoccupied with
questions of the possibility or impossibility of total control.
"...it is not necessary to assume that total control is achieved. It
may be that a very slight shift in the possibilities of a response

at a certain period will produce an important effect."108

Quarton then proposes a scheme for surveying available methods for behavior manipulation. He lists modification of the genetic code, gene selection by controlled mating, nutritional influences, hormones, drugs, neurosurgical interventions, surgery outside the brain, and environmental manipulations. It is this last item which includes the kind of behavior modification we are examining. After his survey, Quarton argues that while there is some disagreement about the present state or the possible development of these various procedures, "... a fairly precise technology exists and will be extensively applied in the next fifty years."109

Quarton then asks how people are reacting to these kinds of technological changes which are becoming increasingly possible. He suggests that:

"... most people seem to be frightened but fascinated. A systematic study of these attitudes might be a very useful tool in making projections in the future."110

Quarton continues by observing that psychiatrists and other professionals appear to be ambivalent about the use of these procedures but that "... one gets the impression that such decision-making bodies have been, on the whole, quite conservative."111

Quarton then sketches some alternative futures in which the extension of behavior modifying procedures would be justified in different ways: the first justification would be by what he calls humanitarian values, which he translates as meaning "... keeping each individual alive and without pain as long as possible even though he has little to live for."112 But there is clearly something amiss with this understanding of humanitarian values. "In spite of the fact that such a society would undoubtedly produce weak individuals incapable of meeting new threats from the environment, there are indications in our present society that suggests trends in this direction."113

Another value justifying the extensive use of behavior modification would be efficacy. But there will be limits set upon this norm, according to Quarton. "Hostility to totalitarian forms of government does exist, however, and suggests in most democratic societies that there will be resistance to this type of use unless there is a radical change in our whole social structure."114

A third logical possibility would be the discouragement of the use of behavior manipulation by encouraging social inefficiency, views sometimes espoused by anarchists or libertarians. Quarton does not believe that this will be a widely held view. He also notes but does not regard as influential those who advocate a "puritanical avoidance of behavior control." He considers it most likely that there will be "multiple parallel developments," in which in various times and places, different values will come to the fore as they are used to justify using or not using a particular behavioral technology.

Quarton concludes with some observations about the rights of individuals related to behavior control.

"The civil rights issues involved in behavior control are very difficult to state with clarity. Since society has been controlling the behavior of the individual throughout history by providing and presenting opportunities for action and by manipulation of reward-punishment systems, it does not make much sense to argue that the control of one individual by another is in itself unethical. It is tempting to say that certain types of behavior control that are novel, efficient, and easily identified - such as deliberate destructive brain surgery-violate the rights of the individual, particularly if they are performed against the wishes of that individual and are irreversible. But this is too easy a solution. Other types of behavior control, such as confinement behind bars, are carried out against the will of the individual, and these may also have some irreversible effects. Groups that have recently explored the dangers inherent in human experimentation have urged that no one be a subject in an experiment unless he gets informed consent. A similar protection might be considered to protect the individual from control. Many doctors and psychologists do not, however, believe informed and free consent is really possible. Many individuals cannot understand the technical details of the procedures to which they are given consent, and agreement after discussion or persuasion is not really free."115

According to Quarton the most difficult issue will be conflict between group and individual objectives.

"The difficulty in making policies concerning behavior-manipulation techniques lies in reaching agreement on social goals, particularly those goals that balance group objectives against the rights of individuals to make certain decisions and to behave in certain limits without interference."116

In many respects, Quarton's discussion is one of the most helpful we have examined. His admonition that discussion should focus on genuine possibilities rather than extravagant speculation is much to the point. His effort to schematize and arrange the several methods of behavior control is helpful. And particularly useful is his typology of the kinds of ethical justifications which are likely to be used for certain kinds of behavior control. It is, I believe, a superb essay in social analysis and social criticism.

Quarton's concluding analysis of the ethical dilemmas in behavior control is also penetrating. He is far less willing to settle for easy answers than were some of the other thinkers we examined.

What we do not find in Quarton's essay, however, is an explicit moral vision and moral principles for guiding decisions about applied behavior modification. That was not, of course, the task to which he set himself. But it is the task to which we must now turn.

F. AN ETHIC FOR BEHAVIOR MODIFICATION

In all the viewpoints examined so far in this chapter--from Skinner to Quarton--we found valuable elements of an ethic for behavior modification. Key issues were identified--the distribution of power, conflicts between individual and social aims, whether the therapist is the agent of society or the individual, and the possible abuses of behavioral technology in the hands of those who would use it for personal gain or unwarranted power. And normative moral visions were present--Skinner's behavioral utopia, and references to democratic social values. But nowhere did we find a fully developed ethical treatment of behavior modification which spelled out a normative moral vision, principles for applying the vision to specific cases, and the necessary technical knowledge. I want to outline such an ethic in the concluding section of this chapter.

1. A Normative Vision:

Since I write as a Christian believer and theologian, my statement of the ultimate moral vision which must be used in developing an ethic for behavior modification is derived from the faith that the God of the universe has made known the content of the human good in the events surrounding the life and teachings and death and resurrection of Jesus of Nazareth. This disclosure is in response to the common human longing for justice in an unjust world, longing for an abiding relationship of love in the midst of transient human relationships, longing for a basis of hope when it is known that all hopes will be cancelled by death.

This disclosure and this longing come together in the vision of God's new age, which suggests a new set of relationships and qualities beginning now in the life of faith, but only imperfectly or fragmentarily realized in the present. So the vision points to an assured future, in which God completes justice, love and hope.

127

Such a vision, formed in symbolic images, is rich in possible meanings for ethical analysis. I want to propose three statements of implication regarding the principles of human relationships required by this vision. These are not the only possible implications of such a normative vision. But they are the kind of implications which will be most helpful in developing an ethic of behavior modification.

First, the dimension of restored justice in the normative vision requires a general principle which affirms that all people must have equitable access to the resources to sustain and enhance life, and to the power by which decisions affecting their lives are made. These lines of access must not be blocked because of environmental or cultural circumstances. Power must be distributed in ways which are especially sensitive to the interests of individuals, small groups, and minorities, against the massive influence of corporate social institutions.

Secondly, the dimension of restored love in the normative vision requires a general principle which affirms universal access to opportunities for education, personal growth and development, and the creation of socially satisfying relationships and institutions. The principle of justice is necessary but not sufficient. There must also be a principle of love which affirms opportunity, growth and relationships which go beyond and are not calculable by justice alone.

Third, the dimension of restored hope in the normative vision requires a general principle which locates the ground of human possibility in God, rather than human effort alone, or some particular dimension of the human personality. The vision of a just and loving world is not just a universal human dream or aspiration. It is grounded in the reality of God. So while striving for the good requires clear thought, hard work, personal sacrifice and suffering, no one of these human activities is "the prescription" for moral improvement. The vision of the good life is already empowered by God. The appropriate human responses are confidence in the ultimate triumph of the good and hard work to achieve as much of that good as possible.

2. *Principles and Guidelines:*

I have now proposed a normative moral vision--God's new age--and three normative statements derived from it, concerning justice, love and hope. We move next to guidelines or principles to be used to relate abstract moral norms to specific cases. These principles or guidelines must be sufficiently general so that they are demonstrably consistent with the guiding moral vision, but also specific enough to use in actual cases of choice. I propose that we need five such principles, dealing with a just distribution of power, assessing likely gains in relation to losses, representative decision-making, enhancement of responsibility, and opportunities for growth. The first three are primarily concerned to protect the principle of justice, the other two express the principle of love. They all reflect the principle of hope, since all point to new human possibilities.

The first is the principle of the just distribution of power. If a proposed program or therapeutic intervention seems likely to maintain or make worse an imbalance of power, the proposed action must be challenged. If, on the other hand, it seems clear that one of the consequences of the proposed intervention or program is a more equal distribution of power, then there can be greater confidence in the ethical propriety of the proposal.

The second principle affirms the need to calculate the proprotion of gains and losses to be experienced in any proposed therapeutic intervention or program. This is often a difficult assessment to make. New possibilities may be over-sold, or may be unrealistically enticing. The familiar is at least secure. It is always difficult to represent the possible losses fairly. They tend to be underestimated by advocates (therapists, friends, etc.), and overestimated by the patients.

The third principle calls for representative participation in decisions about therapeutic interventions or programs. Clearly all of the parties involved in the possible intervention or program need to be represented - the scientist or researcher, the therapist, the therapeutic team, the client or patient or subject population, and persons and institutions which will feel the impact. It is also necessary to find ways to involve the public interest. This is particularly important when decisions may establish precedents having widespread public implications. But even in cases that appear to be purely personal problems, there must be mechanisms by which the public interest can be represented in the decision making process. While such representative participation in decisions about behavioral programs or therapies will be more cumbersome than if they were left in the hands of the scientists and therapists, justice will be better served by increasing participation in the decision making process.

A fourth principle calls for enhancing responsibility. To the extent that a proposed program or therapeutic intervention will enhance the ability of the patient or subject population to assume a greater degree of personal responsibility for the conduct of their lives, such a proposal can be ethically supported. On the other hand, if it seems that responsibility will be reduced or taken away, especially if this reduction is permanent, questions must be raised about the ethical propriety of the proposed program.

The fifth principle calls for programs or therapies which enhance ·personal growth, fulfillment and development. If the only benefit appears to be more efficient management by the controllers, and if there is no way to project growth or change for the client, ethical questions must be raised.

3. *Applications*:

From the normative vision and these five principles of application, we now consider cases of applied behavior modification. I will attempt to show how these principles of application can be used in making decisions about specific instances, and implications for policies and laws. The cases are arranged in order of difficulty, beginning with the easiest and moving to the most difficult.

a. Adult Patients:

These are cases in which persons who are adults seek help with specific behavioral problems by going to behavior modification programs or therapists. In these cases the ethical considerations appear to be the same as with any other therapeutic or educational programs. First, will the proposed program or therapy produce the desired effects? Here the potential client must depend on legal and professional safeguards which govern the claims of the discipline. Secondly, have the customary procedures for securing informed consent been followed? Has the treatment been fully explained? Have the risks and benefits been explained? Have alternative treatment options been discussed? Have the likely length, duration, pain and side effects been explored? And has the client been assured that treatment can be terminated at any time the client might decide to do so?

So long as these customary legal and ethical procedures are observed, behavior therapy should be ethically approved for adults seeking the specific treatment which behavior modification provides. It would be unethical to deny access to behavioral therapy simply because one might be philosophically or religiously opposed to behaviorism or determinism.

b. Severely Retarded and Psychotic Persons:

It is easy to recommend behavior modification with such persons, because nothing else seems to have worked at all, while behavior modification has worked to some degree. These cases include children or adults who are so severely mentally retarded as to require institutional care and basic personal maintenance; severely withdrawn or disturbed children who have been diagnosed as autistic; the most severely disturbed or withdrawn schizophrenic patients who require constant institutional maintenance and restraint; and patients who suffer uncontrollable periods of physical aggression. The principles of weighing gains against losses, and promoting personal enhancement and responsibility (only very modestly improved in such persons) seem

130

to warrant the use of behavior modification methods.

Ethical arguments have been made against aversive or operant methods with any institutionalized person, charging that institutionalization itself is such cruel and unusual punishment that there is no way for any treatment administered during incarceration to be ethical. According to this view, it is ethically preferable to provide only custodial care for these persons, rather than inflicting further indignities such as those entailed in aversive or operant conditioning procedures. This is an important argument, but I believe it is misapplied in this group of cases. It fits other kinds of inmate populations, as I will show later.

While I believe that, in these cases, the positive possibilities of behavior modification clearly outweigh the risks, we still need to emphasize ethical safeguards. It is ethically important that behavior modification not be oversold to the public, professionals, administrators, and the friends and families of these severely retarded or psychotic people. It is easy to build false hopes. The evidence suggests that some of these patients can be conditioned to an improved degree of self care and management. But we are not going to empty the institutions in the foreseeable future.

Another ethical safeguard to be observed in these cases requires care at the point of classification: who decides that a given individual is truly in this severe group of cases, and not in other groups to be discussed later? The third principle of application discussed above would suggest that such decisions would require the participation of the patient, the patient's family, concerned public or private health and welfare officials and professionals, with access to the decision making process by representatives of the public interest. While it is easy to talk abstractly about the severely retarded and disturbed, as though such boundaries were relatively easy to identify, in fact there are many questionable or borderline cases. It is important that such borderline cases be handled with extreme care. The behavior-modification bandwagon may not be the best for all of them.

But if all these safeguards are observed, I believe it is ethically appropriate to use aversive and operant procedures with persons who are so severely disturbed or retarded that they have had little hope of ever having more than an exceedingly bleak custodial existence.

c. Children with Learning and Behavioral Problems:

My concern here is with children who have learning or behavioral disorders which are severe enough to make life clearly difficult for themselves and those around them, but not severe enough to require institutionalization away from the family, the community and the school. Shall we treat these disorders with behavioral technologies?

The laws and customs of our society have reflected the belief that until a child reaches the age of majority, decisions about the child's welfare lie primarily in the hands of the child's parents, guardian, other relatives, or community-appointed custodians. But laws and customs are never static. They grow and change. And one of the changes which is taking place in American society today is a shift toward lowering the age at which responsibility is attributed to children and young people, a shift expressed in laws lowering the age of adult rights and responsibilities; changed laws or procedures for dealing with youthful offenders in the courts; changed attitudes toward the enlistment of young people and children in planning and developing their own educational programs in the school system; and, indeed, changes in the world of merchandizing and advertising which reflect the awareness that youthful tastes and peer pressures have market impact. Actively promoting these changed attitudes and practices are those organizing for "children rights," or "children liberation," and those who advocate greater social control over family life, including required education in parenting, more liberal policies regarding the placement of children in alternative home settings, and the like.

Under such circumstances, it would seem important to begin the process of deciding whether to use behavioral methods for treating learning or behavior difficulties by assessing the degree to which the child's difficulty is primarily disturbing or disruptive to other persons, or whether the child wants to change. If the child needs and wants change in order to feel better, to function better, and to adapt better, then the assessment can proceed to other questions. In any case, the child's own interests must be taken into account.

A second question to be considered is the proportion of expected gains to possible losses. The same kind of care must be used here as with the cases described earlier. It is easy to oversell the value of change and to neglect possible losses, such as the child's loss of trust in adults whose pressure for change can be perceived as a lack of love.

A third ethical safeguard would be the effort to involve the child as much as possible in the process of making the decision, seeking to explain as fully as possible the procedure which is being considered, the expected gains and losses, along with the assurance that the child's own judgment will be taken seriously into account. In fact, the success or failure of a particular therapeutic intervention may hinge on the degree to which the child has thought the

132

matter over and decided not only to cooperate but to work as hard as possible to make the therapeutic program successful.

But even when these safeguards are observed, there are many cases where judgments conflict. The child may not be able or willing to understand, or give consent or commitment to the procedure. Judges, school counselors, teachers, or parents may come to differing and about the worth of some proposed therapeutic program. In such instances of conflict, it would seem especially important to protect the child's interests since the legal and customary weight of power is in the hands of the community, represented by school, court or parents. A desirable mechanism might be a review or advisory panel which would be charged with hearing the conflicting arguments and making recommendations which would seek to support the interests of the child. Such review and appeal procedures already exist in some hospitals and other institutions. Juvenile court and school agencies, as well as professional review committees among behavior therapists, should consider the creation of such appeal and review bodies.

These recommendations about the ethical use of behavior modification for learning or behavioral difficulties are based upon the principles of the cost-benefits ratio and the distribution of power and decision-making. The involvement of the child represents the principles of increased responsibility and personal growth.

d. Children Who are Different:

This group of cases includes children who are "different" to a degree that may concern their teachers, parents, or friends, for example, children and young people who are shy and withdrawn, or who do not participate in social activities, or who are not as aggressive or assertive as some people think they should be. Is it ethically appropriate to recommend (or for parents to require) behavior modification to encourage greater similarity to other children, greater participation with peers, greater participation in class discussion, to become more active and aggressive, or whatever?

Again we must begin with the child, trying to discover how the child feels about being different. That can be hard to determine. Often the child is ambivalent about such differences, sometimes feeling a certain pride and distinction in connection with them, and at other times wishing desperately and urgently that they were not so odd. An important consideration is the degree of helplessness which the child is able to sense and acknowledge, or which can be sensed by those who are close to the child. If the child feels trapped and really wants to change, behavior modification might be an appropriate treatment. But if the child cherishes these differences and does not feel trapped by them, that would indicate not so much a need for behavior modification, as for greater understanding and love.

133

It is difficult in practice to know when you have actually enlisted the child's informed consent, how much that should count, and when the responsible adult must overrule with younger children, where personality formation and language skill limit their ability to reflect on alternatives. And those who are responsible for such decisions often must make them on the basis of confusing or inconclusive information. But the effort to involve the child and give due weight to the child's judgments will surely result in a more ethical outcome than following the tradition which holds that the parents or school or court always know best.

e. Adult Mental Patients:

The next group of cases to be considered consists of adult committed mental patients who are not so clearly or obviously withdrawn, self-destructive, or requiring personal and institutional maintenance as the group considered earlier. These are difficult cases ethically because we have created diagnostic categories for all kinds of mental illness which are socially given labels and socially learned roles. These diagnostic categories allow us to institutionalize and "treat" a great many people who are not likely to harm themselves or society, but who act in one of the ways we have labeled "mental illness." We still do not know what "causes" mental illness. Early relationships, inherited or genetic predispositions, stressful and environmental circumstances, and biochemical processes are studied and claimed to be causes of mental illness. There is a great deal of promising research. And many kinds of treatments have been tried. But we still do not have conclusive research findings. And we usually do not know why certain treatments succeed or fail.

Behavior modification therapies have been successfully demonstrated with certain kinds of mental illness. Severe obsessive-compulsive neuroses have been successfully treated with Joseph Wolpe's systematic desensitization. The typically passive and withdrawn behavior of many mental hospital patients has been significantly changed through token economy programs. And the behaviorists claim, on the basis of their general theory, that what we call mental illness consists of learned behavior. If the symptoms have been learned, they can be unlearned, and new behaviors can be learned in their place.

Does that then mean that those who have charge of institutionalized mental patients also have the right to institute therapeutic programs to "cure" their symptoms without their own consent? Because the court has committed them, have they lost the right to evaluate and refuse treatments which may be proposed for them?

Seymour Halleck, in an article in the *American Journal of Psychiatry*, answers as follows:

134

"I do not feel that there is ever any ethical justification for deceiving the patient. All patients, even the most disturbed, should be informed of what will be done to them, why it will be done, and what effects the treatment is likely to have. If after having such information, the patient still does not consent to treatment, coercive treatment is justified only if the following sets of conditions are met:

"First, the patient must be judged to be dangerous to himself or others. In the case of the civilly committed patients, this judgment has often been made in the process of commitment.

"Second, those who are providing treatment must believe there is a reasonable probability that treatment will be of benefit to the patient as well as to those around him.

"Third, the patient must be judged to be incompetent to evaluate the necessity for treatment."[117]

Halleck acknowledges that these conditions are sometimes difficult to judge, but that all three must be met before coercive treatment is employed.

Recent court decisions concerning the treatment of the involuntary patient have broadened the safeguards for the individual against coercive or intrusive treatment. Ethically we need to observe Halleck's proposed procedures in order to counteract the tendency to treat committed and institutionalized mental patients as less than fully human beings.

I would add an additional safeguard to Halleck's list. The committed mental patient not only needs to be informed about proposed treatment and give consent. There must also be an independent review and appeals procedure available to the mental patient, who might feel that undue coercion was employed even though the principle of informed consent was observed. Doctors, hospital administrators and courts must have access to such an appeal body, but cannot control it. The patient's right to legal counsel must be honored in these procedures, including the provision of legal counsel at public expense for indigent patients.

f. Adult Prisoners:

Next we inquire about behavior modification for adult felons, whether serving prison terms, on parole, living in half-way houses,

135

or in whatever other treatment or rehabilitation program the court
may have prescribed. Is it ever ethical to prescribe or require
behavior modification for such persons?

Controversy over behavior modification programs for "hard core"
prisoners in federal institutions led to an investigation of
"Individual Rights and the Federal Role in Behavior Modification,"
by the Judiciary Committee of the United States Senate, a study
which was completed and published in November, 1974. This report
observes that there has been an increase in litigation in the field
of behavior modification in recent years due largely to two factors:
(1) an increase in a number of behavior modification programs in
prisons and mental institutions; and (2) an increased willingness on
the part of the courts to drop their former "hands-off doctrine and
begin scrutinizing treatment and living conditions in prisons and
mental institutions."[118]

The committee report goes on to suggest that "... the broad
question becomes whether institutionally confined individuals have
rights to or against various methods of treatment or rehabilitation."[119]

In summarizing court cases dealing with the relevant Constitutional issues, the report notes that:

"... some courts have recently held, first, that
constitutionally guaranteed rights to due process
and personal privacy, as well as first and eighth
amendment rights, do apply to institutionalized
populations; and second, at a minimum, that informed
consent is required before certain experimental
techniques are used in these populations. Some courts
have gone even further in holding that because truly
voluntary consent is required before a person is subjected to radical experimentation, as a matter of
law and involuntarily detained person cannot give
the required consent."[120]

In attempting to judge among the kinds of behavior modification
being employed, the committee report concluded as follows:

"Of all the methods of behavior modification
presently being employed in the United States,
positive reinforcement is perhaps the most benign.
But as with all other forms of behavior modification,
positive reinforcements seeks to restructure personality through artifically applied techniques."[121]

Both of these issues - the question of consent in the treatment
of involuntary prisoners or patients and the suggestion that operant

or positive conditioning is more legally and ethical supportable than other methods - were discussed in a debate which took place in the pages of *Hospital and Community Psychiatry*. In the February, 1968, issue of that journal, R. Joseph Lucero, David J. Vail, and John Scherber described a workshop held in Minnesota in March of 1967 to arrive at humane guidelines for the use of various conditioning methods in state public welfare institutions. They described the workshop as arriving at three major recommendations: "Aversive reinforcement is never to be used in a general program for groups of patients. However, in an unusual individual case in which physical abuse of self or others is otherwise unchangeable, aversive reinforcement methods may be used...."[122] The authors specify those conditions under which aversive methods might be used, including the provision that the procedures would have to be performed by a qualified professional person, the decision to use this treatment would need to be cleared with the medical director of the institution and with the Mental Health Medical Policy Committee of the Department of Public Welfare.

The second recommendation stated:

> "Deprivation is never to be used. No patient is to be deprived of expected goods and services and ordinary rights, including free movement for his limbs, that he had before the program started. In addition, deficit rewarding must be avoided; that is, rewards must not consist of the restoration of objects or privileges that were taken away from the patient or that he should have had to begin with. The ban against deficit rewarding includes the use of tokens to gain or regain such objects or privileges.

> "Positive reinforcement is the only conditioning technique to be used, with the exception of aversive methods in the approved individual cases noted above."[123]

In the July, 1968 issue of the same periodical, several writers responded to this set of guidelines. Nathan B. Miron argues that:

> "the electric shock used in such cases [aversive methods] is a very low amperage and is usually from flashlight batteries; the shock, although painful, is not much more painful than some injections, and is probably less 'brutal' than electrical convulsive therapy and psychosurgery...."

> "The alternative to such a use of contingent punishment may be a life spent in restraint."[124]

Then Miron defends deprivation and token-based programs:

> "In their attack on the use of deprivation and
> tokens in operant conditioning programs, the Minnesota
> workshop participants ignored the fact that we all live
> under a similar economic system. Without deprivation
> there can be little or no positive reinforcements."125

Miron argues his case in this way:

> "What of the patient's civil liberties? How can it
> be ethical to prohibit the use of devices that can
> result in successful placement of chronic patients in
> the community? The real deprivation with which we
> should be concerned - the one most ethically suspect-is
> the deliberate deprivation of potential benefits to
> the patients, when the alternative clearly amounts to
> a life sentence in a mental institution."126

In the same issue of *Hospital and Community Psychiatry*, Delwin D.
Cahoon criticizes the Minnesota guidelines for not balancing risks
against possible outcomes. "It is unprecedented in considering
professional ethics to insist that a whole class of techniques of
proved effectiveness be prohibited because the techniques can be
misapplied."127

And in a final brief response to these criticisms, Lucero and
Vail suggest that their critics

> "...are naive, for they miss the point. Our article
> refers to a public statement drawn up as a guideline
> to public policy for carrying out a public responsi-
> bility.... thus, it is aimed at a level that is
> different from, and at times in conflict with, the
> level of individual case management or case research."128

The ethical principles I am advocating would suggest that we
support Lucero, Vail and Scherber in this debate. Everything about
involuntary commitment or incarceration says that rights and power
nave been stripped from the individual. While the safety of the
society and indeed the safety of the prisoner may require segregation
and institutionalization, it does not appear to be in the interests
of the prisoner or society to institute coercive behavioral modification programs at the further expense of individual dignity and
rights. If there is any hope for rehabilitation, it must surely lie
in the direction of empowerment and the enhancement of responsibility,
not a further power game played by the strong against the defenseless.

To be given behavior modification, the prisoner should examine the proposed therapeutic program and its promised benefits. If the prisoner consents, therapy can commence. But if the prisoner declines, that decision must be honored and protected. Review and appeal procedures must be available to prisoners as well as mental patients and juvenile offenders.

Without such genuinely informed consent, it is likely that coercive programs of therapy or treatment will "work" only so long as the patient or prisoner behaves "appropriately" in order to please the therapist or parole officer. That is a familiar "reality" in correctional programs and institutions. Patients and prisoners learn what they have to do to get along inside and to get out as soon as possible, and they do it. But such "adaptations" ordinarily do not amount to real change.

g. Total Community Behavior Modification:

The final class of cases in the ethics of behavior modification concern attempt to design a total human community or network employing the principles of behavior modification. What are the ethical guidelines governing such efforts? For existing institutions or networks - schools, correctional systems, community services, business or industrial firms -- the principal ethical guideline would be the consent of the persons involved after a study of the likely effects of such a program. Care would need to be taken against the temptation of administrators to "try out" such programs on their unsuspecting employees, clients, or pupils. Such "secret" efforts are soon enough figured out, and the credibility of administrators may suffer irreparable damage.

There are also efforts to create entirely new communities based on behavior modification principles-rural or urban communes, cooperative craft and business ventures, and the life. One of the best known is the effort to create a *Walden Two* type commune in Virginia, Twin Oaks.[129] Ethical guidelines for such total community formation should scrupulously safeguard the rights of all commune members to participate in communal decisions (rather than leaving it to the benign administrators as in Skinner's *Walden Two*), and should include clear and publicly supported procedures for entering and leaving communal life, so that perfectionistic expectations and guilt are not allowed to control attitudes about joining and leaving.

While not properly a part of the ethics of behavior modification, there is, I believe, ethical as well as legal warrant for the neighbors of such a communal venture to be supporting and understanding, rather than suspicious and hostile. Our whole society may have much to learn from such experiments.

139

F. SUMMARY AND CONCLUSIONS

In this chapter I have explored the ethics of applied behavior modification. I began with an exposition of the three elements in ethical analysis: fundamental moral norms or visions; principles or guidelines for relating fundamental moral visions to concrete cases; and technical information about actual uses of behavior modification.

In examining ethical aspects of the debate between Skinner and his critics, I tried to show that while Skinner articulates a certain kind of moral vision, and while it shares formal utopian characteristics with a Christian vision, there is so much that is logically and ethically questionable that we dare not approve it. I also suggested that Skinner's critics, in their attacks on his philosophy and ethics, had diverted public attention from the more urgent and complex ethical questions arising in applied behavior modification.

We then looked at what a number of behaviorists have to say about the ethics of behavior modification. We also looked at three religious or philosophical evaluations. We found penetrating and sensitive insights in that literature. In much of that discussion, we could make out a fundamental moral vision which is derived from values identified with modern culture and democratic political philosophy. But there was not a sufficiently developed normative moral vision which went beyond specifically modern and Western values, and there was not sufficient attention to the procedures for analyzing cases from an ethical standpoint.

I then proposed a Christian moral vision employing the core metaphor of God's new age, with implications for justice, love and hope. Then I developed five principles or guidelines for relating this normative moral vision to the practice of behavior modifications.

In considering seven kinds of applied behavior modification using these principles, I arrived at the following conclusions:

1. For adults desiring to change, behavior modification can be ethically approved if the usual guidelines for professional self-regulation and informed consent are followed.

2. For severely retarded and psychotic persons, behavior modification (even aversive procedures) can be approved if the decisions are truly representative and if great care is taken in diagnosing "severe" cases.

3. For children with behavioral or learning problems, applied behavior modification should endeavor to enlist the child's consent and commitment. Short of achieving

consent, responsible adults may still have to make the decision. Appeal-review mechanisms should be available.

4. For children who are different, the child's consent and commitment are required. Without consent, the anticipated losses probably outweigh any gains.

5. For adult mental patients, especially those committed by court action, informed consent must be obtained to begin behavior modification programs. Review-appeal mechanisms should be available to patients, along with legal counsel.

6. For adult felons, behavior modification requires informed consent, with the same rights to appeal-review procedures and legal counsel.

7. For total institutional or network efforts to apply behavior modification, there must be full participation in the decision-making process by all persons whose lives will be affected. For communes, this same right of access to decision-making is vital, along with fair and public procedures for entry and exit.

While I have tried to demonstrate the foundation of these conclusions in a Christian moral vision, I trust that it is evident that other moral assumptions may yield similar conclusions, so that there is much common ground for religious and philosophical approaches to the ethics of behavior modification.

And I do not believe the restrictions noted above will unduly interfere with research and progress in behavior modification. Most behavior modification professionals with whom I have discussed these matters clearly affirm the need to enlist the client's consent and commitment. Covert manipulation either does not work at all or is far less effective.

NOTES FOR CHAPTER IV

[1] B. F. Skinner, *Beyond Freedom and Dignity*, 130.

[2] *Ibid.*, 99.

[3] B. F. Skinner, *Science and Human Behavior*, 1.

[4] *Ibid.*, 5.

[5] *Ibid.*, 446.

[6]*Beyond Freedom and Dignity*, 6.

[7]*Ibid.*, 131.

[8]*Ibid.*, 143.

[9]*Ibid.*, 163.

[10]*Ibid.*, 164.

[11]B. F. Skinner, *About Behaviorism*, 211.

[12]B. F. Skinner, *Walden Two*, 263.

[13]*Ibid.*, 264.

[14]*Ibid.*, 268.

[15]*Ibid.*

[16]Joseph Wood Krutch, *The Measure of Man* (Indianapolis: Bobbs-Merrill Company, Inc., 1953), 59.

[17]*Ibid.*, 75.

[18]*Ibid.*, 87.

[19]*Ibid.*, 91-92.

[20]B. F. Skinner in "Some Issues Concerning a Control of Human Behavior: a Symposium," *Science*, vol. 124, 30 November 1956, 264.

[21]Arthur Koestler, *The Ghost in the Machine*, (New York: The Macmillan Company, 1967), 17.

[22]*Ibid.*, 202.

[23]Peter G. Stalman, "The Limits of Behaviorism: A Review Essay of B. F. Skinner's Social and Political Thought," *American Political Science Review*, LXIX, March, 1975, No. 1, 203.

[24]*Ibid.*, 206.

[25]Patrick Bateson in *Applications of Behavior Modification*, ed. by Travis Thompson and William S. Dockens III, (New York: Academic Press, 1975), 488.

[26]*Ibid.*, 501.

[27]*Ibid.*, 505.

[28]Philip H. Scribner, "Escape from Freedom and Dignity," *Ethics*, Vol. 83, No. 1, October, 1972, 13-35.

[29]Willard Gaylin, "Skinner Redux," *Harper's Magazine*, October, 1973, 55.

[30]*Ibid.*

[31]*Ibid.*, 56.

[32]William R. Morrow and Harvey L. Gochros, "Misconceptions Regarding Behavior Modification," *The Social Service Review*, September, 1970, 301.

[33]Anne B. Smith, "Humanism and Behavior Modification," *The Elementary School Journal*, November, 1973, Vol. 74, No. 2, 60.

[34]D. A. Begelman, "Ethical Issues in Behavior Control," *Journal of Nervous and Mental Disease*, 156, No. 6, June, 1973, 414.

[35]Elizabeth Hall, *From Pigeons to People* (Boston: Houghton-Mifflin Co., 1975), 112.

[36]*Ibid.*, 118.

[37]*Ibid.*

[38]Herbert Keleman, "Manipulation of Human Behavior," *Journal of Social Issues*, April, 1965, Vol. XXI, No. 2, 33-34.

[39]Leonard Krasner, *Ibid.*, 17.

[40]*Ibid.*, 22.

[41]*Ibid.*, 23.

[42]*Ibid.*

[43]*Ibid.*, 24.

[44]Leonard Krasner, "Behavior Modification - Values and Training: The Perspective of a Psychologist" in *Behavior Therapy, Appraisal and Status*, ed. by Cryil Franks (New York: McGraw-Hill Book Co., 1969), 541.

[45]*Ibid.*, 542.

[46]*Ibid.*

[47]*Ibid.*

[48]Albert Bandura, *Principles of Behavior Modification*, (New York: Holt, Rinehart and Winston, Inc., 1969), 85.

[49]*Ibid.*, 87.

[50]Leonard P. Ullmann, "Behavior Therapy as Social Movement," in Franks, op.cit., 509.

[51]*Ibid.*, 517.

[52]*Ibid.*, 519.

[53]*Ibid.*, 520.

[54]*Ibid.*, 521.

[55]*Ibid.*, 523.

[56]Margaret E. Lloyd in *Issues in Evaluating Behavior Modification*, ed. W. Scott Wood (Champaign: Research Press, 1975), 20.

[57]Jon E. Krapfl, *Ibid.*, 234.

[58]Stephanie B. Stolz, *Ibid.*, 243.

[59]Robert Neville, "Ethical and Philosophical Issues of Behavior Control," paper #804 published by the Institute of Society, Ethics and the Life Sciences, Hastings-on-Hudson, New York, 1972, 4.

[60]*Ibid.*, 5.

[61]*Ibid.*, 8.

[62]James G. Holland, "Ethical Considerations in Behavior Modification," *Current Ethical Issues in Mental Health*, (Rockville, Md.: N.I.M.H., 1973), 24.

[63]*Ibid.*, 25.

[64]*Ibid.*, 29.

[65]*Ibid.*, 30.

[66]I. J. Barrish, "Ethical Issues and Answers to Behavior Modification," *Corrective and Social Psychiatry and Journal of Behavior Technology Methods and Therapy*, Vol. 20, No. 4, 1974, 31.

[67]*Ibid.*, 32.

[68]*Ibid.*

[69]*Ibid.*, 33.

[70]Perry London, *Behavior Control*, (New York: Harper and Row, 1969), 5-6.

[71]*Ibid.*, 16.

[72]*Ibid.*, 25.

[73]*Ibid.*, 156.

[74]*Ibid.*, 170.

[75]*Ibid.*, 173.

[76]*Ibid.*, 184.

[77]*Ibid.*, 192-193.

[78]*Ibid.*, 199.

[79]*Ibid.*, 201.

[80]*Ibid.*, 208.

[81]*Ibid.*, 213.

[82]*Ibid.*

[83]*Ibid.*, 214.

[84] *Ibid.*, 215.

[85] *Ibid.*, 216.

[86] Israel Goldiamond, "Toward a Constructional Approach to Social Problems," Behaviorism, Spring, 1974, 7.

[87] *Ibid.*, 14.

[88] *Ibid.*, 24.

[89] *Ibid.*

[90] *Ibid.*, 46.

[91] *Ibid.*, 48.

[92] *Ibid.*, 65.

[93] Ronald G. Alexander, "Can A Christian Ethic Condone Behavior Modification?", *Religion in Life*, Summer, 1976, 193.

[94] Ronald G. Alexander, "Toward a Moral Criterion for Use by Behavior Modification," Unpublished paper, 8.

[95] *Ibid.*, 10.

[96] *Ibid.*, 13.

[97] *Ibid.*, 14.

[98] Bernard Häring, *Ethics of Manipulation*, (New York: The Seabury Press, 1975), 11.

[99] *Ibid.*, 70.

[100] *Ibid.*

[101] *Ibid.*, 115.

[102] *Ibid.*, 120-121.

[103] *Ibid.*

[104] *Ibid.*, 123.

[105]*Ibid.*, 125.

[106]*Ibid.*, 129.

[107]Gardner C. Quarton, "Deliberate Efforts to Control Human Behavior and Modify Personality," *Daedalus*, Summer, 1967, Vol. 96, No. 3, 837.

[108]*Ibid.*, 839.

[109]*Ibid.*, 846.

[110]*Ibid.*, 847.

[111]*Ibid.*, 848.

[112]*Ibid.*, 850.

[113]*Ibid.*

[114]*Ibid.*

[115]*Ibid.*, 852.

[116]*Ibid.*

[117]Seymour Halleck, "Legal and Ethical Aspects of Behavior Control," *The American Journal of Psychiatry*, Vol. 131, 1974, 382.

[118]"Individual Rights and the Federal Role in Behavior Modification," Committee of Judiciary, U. S. Senate, Ninety Third Congress, Second Session, November, 1974, 3.

[119]*Ibid.*, 4.

[120]*Ibid.*, 10.

[121]*Ibid.*, 120.

[122]R. Joseph Lucero, David J. Vail, John Scherber, "Regulating Operant Conditioning Programs," *Hospital and Community Psychiatry*, Vol. 19, No. 2, February, 1968, 53.

[123]*Ibid.*, 53-54.

[124]Nathan B. Miron, "The Primary Ethical Consecration," *Hospital and Community Psychiatry*, Vol. 19, No. 7, July, 1968, 226.

[125]*Ibid.*, 227.

[126]*Ibid.*

[127]*Ibid.*, 229.

[128]*Ibid.*, 232.

[129]Kathleen Kinkade, A *Walden Two Experiment* (New York: William Morrow and Company, Inc., 1973).

CHAPTER V

THE CHURCHES AND BEHAVIOR MODIFICATION

If it is true, as I argued in chapter 3, that a behaviorist explanation help us understand many aspects of human experience; and if it is the case, as I argued in chapter 4, that behavior modification can be ethically approved in many situations if safeguards are observed, then we should expect religious institutions to be appropriating these insights and practices. But that does not seem to be happening. Why not?

One plausible answer would be the inherent conservatism of all religious institutions, which causes them to look primarily to their own traditional teachings for insight, not to the worldly disciplines, or which at least makes the process of incorporating worldly wisdom exceedingly slow. But that answer is not sufficient to account for the neglect of behavior modification in the moderate and liberal religious bodies, where other kinds of modern psychology have been enthusiastically, even uncritically embraced. Freudian, neo-Freudian, Rogerian, Gestalt, transactional and human potential psychologies have had a massive impact in church life. Why not behavior modification?

Phillip Huckaby, a United Methodist minister in Alabama, raised these same questions in an article in the *Journal of Pastoral Care,* in the December, 1975 issue. Mr. Huckaby noted that while behavioral psychology is an established major school in American psychology, the religious response to behavioral psychology has been negligible. He looks at several areas of church life which ought to show some kind of influence--pastoral counseling, Christian education and theology. He observes that:

"... the literature on pastoral counseling since 1968 has indicated little evidence of incorporating behavioral techniques or concepts into pastoral counseling. Of twenty books surveyed in this period, only five carried any reference to behavior modification. Of these, one repudiated the use of these procedures. Another made reference to Skinner's learning theory and to the value of behavior therapy without discussing it and with a caution about its use. A third listed a reference to the usefulness of one behavioral technique, reciprocal inhibition but did not discuss them. Only one book recommended behavior modification as a viable methodology for pastoral counseling and provided some guidelines for its use."[1]

In examining the literature of Christian education, Huckaby notes that "... of eight books (published since 1970) surveyed, only one contained any reference to behavior modification and that was to distinguish the author's position from behavioral psychology."[2]

In examining any theological critique of behavior modification, Huckaby finds that most responses consisted of book reviews of Skinner's *Beyond Freedom and Dignity*. And most of these reviews reacted

"... to the theoretical implications of Skinner's proposal for the Christian understanding of man and for the picture of the world which his techniques would create. Few of these reviewers acknowledged any positive contribution of operant conditioning, Skinner's formulation on which behavior therapy is based."[3]

Huckaby concludes by speculating about this neglect and the generally negative reaction where any notice is taken.

"Perhaps a major reason is in the current orientation of pastoral counseling which is built upon psychological principles derived from Freud and Rogers. This is the basic orientation of pastoral psychology. Most contemporary religious psychology utilizes the medical model. This model focuses upon the inner dynamics of the person, and regards what is expressed as symptomatic of the problems existing within the person's consciousness or subconscious life. Behavioral psychology takes an almost diametircally opposed approach by treating the behaviors which are involved in the problems. The inner states and consciousness are ignored, though not necessarily denied. This has led to the accusation that behavior therapy is only symptom treatment and that it does not deal with the real cause of the problem, which lies within the person."[4]

I believe that Huckaby's statement about the dependence of pastoral counseling and pastoral psychology on a medical model derived from Freud and Rogers is essentially correct, and helps explain the neglect of behavioral psychology and behavior modification. But Huckaby does not try to find the deeper reasons for this bias. I would suggest two reasons: First, the Freud-Rogers-human potential theories seem more congruent with the cheerful, optimistic outlook which prevails in many religious bodies where sin has fallen into disfavor. Secondly, these therapeutic techniques seem easier to learn and apply, and their emphasis on the responsibility of the client comfortably absolves the pastoral counselor of responsibility or guilt.

This whole bias for a certain kind of psychology urgently needs to be reassessed. I believe that religious institutions can profit from behaviorism and behavior modification without losing gains already made in pastoral psychology and religious education with the help of the Freud-Rogers-human potential psychology.

In this chapter we will be examining four areas of religious institutional life where behavior modification has something to offer: theology, social action, pastoral counseling, and religious education. There is not much literature to survey, but we will look at what there is, for signposts pointing to further developments.

A. BEHAVIOR MODIFICATION AND THEOLOGY

As Huckaby observed in his essay, there were a number of reviews, review articles, and brief editoral comments in religious periodicals shortly after the publication of Skinner's *Beyond Freedom and Dignity*. Most of these reviews and editorials were critical, because of Skinner's apparent rejection of human freedom, and a directing spirit or soul. So these reviewers did not find positive implications of behavior modification for the faith of the church.

An exception to this general rule was a short article by Russell C. Llewellyn in *Psychology and Theology*, in July, 1973. While Llewellyn points out, like the other critics, irreconcilable conflicts between Skinner and Christian belief, he does try to identify some points in common: first, he suggests that there is a similarity between reinforcement theory and what Llewellyn calls the "dualism" of Christianity, which is the conflict between good and evil. What he means is that the Christian faith requires moral purity in a world (environment) which is full of temptations (negative reinforcers). Against these negative, worldly reinforcers are the positive moral reinforcers of Christianity.

Llewellyn identifies another similarity. "... a point of agreement is reached between contingency management and Christian theology in that both claim behavior is important."[5] Behavior is important of course, but one would think that two thousand years of Christian faith and morals would not need behavior modification to confirm the fact that behavior is important. But Llewellyn may be making a more important point than he realizes. Behavior has been neglected or viewed as consequent upon faith in the whole "evangelical" tradition, from Paul through Augustine, Luther and Calvin, and into the modern Neo-orthodox theologies. To view good works as flowing from true faith may be theologically correct, but may also have resulted in the loss of practical moral guidance in how to live, behaviorally.

There are other dimensions of the Christian heritage, of course, which have maintained an emphasis upon behavior or the works of faith. The traditions of self discipline, penance, spiritual advice and direction and disciplined communal Christian living, such as in monasticism, are some examples. What Llewellyn may be suggesting is that we need to reclaim these historic Christian behavioral traditions to guide Christian living today, and not rely so exclusively upon an inner state of belief which is supposed to govern what people do. The lesson of behavioral psychology and behavioral modification is clearly the lesson that environmental or external reinforcers are constantly involved in shaping how we act.

Another attempt to use behavioral psychology for theology appears in an article by James H. Reynierse in *Psychology and Theology*, in the summer issue of 1975, where behavioral psychology is used as an interpretive model for discovering new meanings in scripture, in this instance, the Book of Job from the Old Testament. Reynierse employs the behavioral explanation of depression as "learned helplessness," as developed by Seligman,[6] and attempts to demonstrate that "...there is an almost perfect correspondence between the events that led to the maladaptive depression of Job and the necessary experimental conditions which produce 'learned helplessness' in the laboratory."[7] These conditions, according to the work of Seligman and others, appear when events are neither predictable nor controllable. If that situation lasts long enough, the experimental subject (animal or human being) reacts by developing clinical symptoms which we call depression.

As the story of Job unfolds, Job's friends provide a parallel to Wolpe's therapeutic procedure of systematic desensitization. When God addresses Job from the whirlwind in the concluding section of the book, it is very much like the behavioral method of implosion or flooding, developed by Thomas Stampfl (discussed in Chapter 2). God's address to Job "... is a continuous, unrelenting assault which Job cannot escape."[8] This kind of use of psychological categories to interpret passages of scripture and other aspects of religious history is a familiar procedure. The modern era is full of attempts to "explain" biblical miracles, visions, conversions, the lives of the saints using scientific methods. However, ingenious or preposterous, these efforts are flawed by the underlying assumption that the original event is meaningless unless it can be rescued by translation into modern (acceptable) scientific explanations. So we should surely not treat Reynierse's essay as the discovery which finally explains the mystery of the Book of Job. But if we can agree to preserve the original message of Job and its place in the faith of Israel, we might still entertain the possibility that Reynierse is onto something interesting, that if behavioral explanations are better than other explanations for some events, we might be willing to agree that the manner in which Job's counseling "worked", first at the hands of his friends and then at the hands of God, was indeed because of the behavioral methods used.

The most substantively theological analysis of behavior modification published to date is Michael Novak's essay, "Is He Really a Grand Inquisitor?," which appears in the collection of essays entitled, *Beyond the Punitive of Society*. Novak suggests a similarity between Skinner and the death of God theologians.

> "... Skinner demythologizes autonomy, the individual,
> freedom and dignity in conscious parody of an earlier
> demythologizing of Creator and Redeemer. As God died,
> so now must the autonomous individual. It is not
> surprising that reaction against his work is religious
> in intensity."[9]

Novak goes on to suggest several ways in which Skinner's work can be useful in theological construction. First he notes that "... Professor Skinner's emphasis upon the social character of human existence (versus individualism) is ..., from a theological point of view, confirmatory of a well-established trend...."[10] Novak is arguing here that modern theology has tried to go beyond the radical individualism of Christian life and faith which has characterized so much of modern Western thought. There is a new emphasis on the person-in-community, as an antidote to individualism. Thus Novak finds Skinner's environmentalism helpful in nurturing this new emphasis, which goes against the prevalent currents of subjectivism, privatism and individualism.

Novak suggests another point of congeniality between Skinner's thought and certain Christian ideas.

> "A second reason why many theologians find Skinner's
> position congenial concerns Christian images of
> Providence and Grace. To speak merely from a Thomist
> standpoint... nothing of good that a human does is
> deserving of credit; everything is grace... man's
> freedom, in this view, is thoroughly conditioned:
> (1) no one chooses his parents, economic situation
> childhood setting, nation of origin, or historical
> era; (2) no one chooses his natural (we would say,
> genetic) endowment; (3) no one chooses the networks
> of circumstance in which he finds himself, or the laws
> or contingencies governing their behavior; and (4)

no one chooses the insights, assumptions, or inspira-
tions that emerge in his or her consciousness."[11]

This emphasis upon a grace-filled world, a world in which grace is
mediated through all of the common events of history, society and
other circumstances, which Novak identifies with the Thomist tradition, strikes a different chord from the emphasis of Luther or
Calvin on the mediation of grace through the decision of faith.

"... the intellectual structure of Skinner's world view -
with God left out - is rather more like that of Aquinas
than like that of Luther or Calvin. For Aquinas grace
operates (except in the rarest cases) through the
ordinary contingencies and processes of nature, through
"secondary causes" - there are always "behavioral processes to be taken into account."[12]

Novak then identifies a third appreciation of Skinner's work
for theology.

"... the third theme that Christians may find attractive
in Skinner's work is his emphasis on earthly, bodily,
environmental supports. Christianity is an incarnational
religion. The dominant symbol through which it shapes
perception is that God does not appear as God (pure,
dazzling, overpowering, and inescapable) but as flesh.
The Godly way is not by way of escape from flesh, but
through the flesh."[13]

Novak also defends Skinner against the charge that Skinner's
behaviorally controlled Utopian community would destroy the individual.

"In a powerful way, the wisdom of the Benedictines -
who have successfully been building and multiplying
Utopian communities since the sixth century - is a sort
of Skinnerism in advance. ... and, ironically, their
high social emphasis on "reinforcers" produces not
uniformity but a highly developed individuality, as
anyone who had known the angularity of individual
Benedictines can attest."[14]

But Novak is not an uncritical advocate of Skinner. In this
same essay, he identified one of the chief defects:

"If Skinner did not claim so much for his technology
of behavior we might be writing to concede him more.
So complex is 'environment,' so variable are the
'controls,' that in assenting to the fundamental
Skinnerian principle that environment controls
behavior, we do not know what we are agreeing to.

"Whatever the preliminary successes in elementary, rudimentary behavior, the fascinating complications of human behavior - not yet exhausted even in song and fiction - have hardly yet been addressed by science. Shall a science of behavior arrive before the Parousia, the 'end of time'? To trust in it requires great faith.

"In these respects, Skinner's work is more like theology than like science. The burgeoning of such speculation, if it continues, may well bring about from an unexpected direction, that rebirth of metaphysics that accompanies each new cultural age."15

This last tantalizing hint, that behavior modification may force our culture to rethink basic questions, should not to be neglected by theologians, who are always under the mandate to be rethinking the faith in light of changing conditions in the world in which faith lives.

Another major theological essay dealing with the impact of behavior modification on theology and the churches appeared in the *Chicago Theological Seminary Register,* in the September issue of 1971. This entire issue was devoted to the church and behavior modification, and is divided into two major sections: an initial essay by Richard C. Schlotman exploring the theological implications of behavior modification, and then a report on applied behavior modification in the youth program of a suburban church. We will save the report for later in the chapter.

Schlotman states his viewpoint in the theological essay this way:

"It is the thesis of this paper that current Behavior Modification approaches give us powerful and responsible tools for the shaping process, when combined with theological interpretation and prescription. These tools may be used constructively or destructively depending upon the goals and norms, which must be formulated in dialogue between the theologians and behavioral scientists."16

Schlotman argues that we are in a time when two kinds of forms of church life are in contention: Church life in which forms are dominant, that is, church life in which the articles of faith, the rules of behavior, the structuring of religious institutions and the locations of roles within them are all formalized and maintained; and the form of church life in which dynamics are dominant over forms, breaking forms and creating new forms, that is, church life in which there is characteristically high level of energetic activity, attributed to new insights or new manifestations of the Holy Spirit, with the result that form-dominant religious institutions are being threatened and challenged. Schlotman sees hope for renewal in the churches in the movements characterized by high dynamism, but is fearful that church organizations in which forms are dominant will not readily adapt themselves to these new dynamisms, with the result that new religious institutions will be created, rather than renewing the older ones.

It is in the dialogue between behavioral science and theology that Schlotman hopes to show that one can develop behavioral norms for the life of the Christian community which will resolve this conflict between form-dominant church organizations and dynamic-dominant movements.

The major part of Schlotman's essay is devoted to developing a set of categories for understanding types of religious behavior which might be explained and taught using behavior modification principles. He identifies the _relating_ dimension, which includes caring, confirming and giving; the _reality-orienting_ dimension, which includes data processing, testing and responsible commitments; the dimension of _community participation_, which includes involvement, bending and shaping; and the _death-life_ dimension, which includes "facing the impass," courageous action, and accepting the acceptance of God. Schlotman suggests that all of these dimensions of Christian behavior might be learned and taught using behavioral methods.

> "The impressive evidence regarding human learning and the powerful techniques constituting the armamentum of the Neo-Behaviorist must be complimented by a theological sense of ultimacy and specificity. I am convinced that theology is unprepared for this kind of specificity and power to define and implement norms. We have too much engaged in the Prophetic (form-breaking) task and in the Pastor/Priest (dynamic-enabling) task, but now we must turn to the equally responsible Government task of shaping the forms into which the new dynamic can flow."[17]

Scholtman's provocative essay is more suggestive than fully developed in specifying how theologians and behavioral scientists might conduct their dialogue. His statement that theology deals with ultimate aims and norms while behavioral science deals with techniques is helpful but only to a certain point. Psychological orientations, like religious faiths, presuppose distinctive ways of looking at all of reality. It is not always that easy to specify knowledge or techniques which can be loosened from a particular metaphysical context and taken over into a Christian theological setting without doing violence to theology or science. Scholtman does not seem to be aware of this difficulty attending the dialogue which he proposes. He seems to view behavioral scientists as no more than technicians, whom we can employ to achieve theologically desirable aims. Dialogue, however, suggests a more collegial enterprise, dealing with fundamental questions.

In Chapter 3, I suggested that dialogue about the will and the limits it sets on behavioral explanation might be fruitful. I hope that others will be prompted to enter such a dialogue. Surely there are many ways theologically to approach the question of the impact of environment on human behavior, and the place of God and God's activity in those relationships.

B. SOCIAL ACTION

Every religious institution, whether it be a local congregation, a denomination, or a specialized agency, has some kind of impact on its society. Many of these effects are unintended, such as when silence on a particular issue (for principled reasons) is interpreted as agreement with things as they are, or when a public stand on controversial issues harms rather than helps the cause, because people are angry about religion trying to control their lives.

But there are also the intended effects, and the implied theories of how religious institutions should be related to society, ranging from extreme forms of withdrawal to religious dominance and control. (H. Richard Niebuhr has definitively described the options in *Christ and Culture*).

Many religious denominations have social action programs, with professional staff, boards and study groups, documents and policy papers, aimed at assisting their constituents in relating faith to social issues.

I have not found that any of these social action agencies are dealing with behavior modification as a significant social issue in our time. Individual authors who are studying and writing in biomedical ethics, -like Bernhard Häring's book on the ethics of manipulation, which we examined in the last chapter, or Kenneth Vaux and James B. Nelson - have looked at behavior control. But these discussions tend to focus on medical rather than environmental control methodologies, like psychosurgery and brain implants, mood-and perception-altering drugs, and punitive techniques.

Observers of American religious institutions have suggested that we are living in a time when there is a reaction against social activism and a return to inward, subjective, and spiritual forms of piety. If this is true, it would seem unlikely that behavior modification will get the attention it deserves, when it must compete for the residue of privatistic religious social concern with such dramatic difficulties as scarce food resources, energy, race relations, third world concerns, justice for oppressed peoples, women's issues, and human sexuality.

Even though these chances may be slim, it should certainly be hoped that socially concerned persons and agencies in religious institutions would look at social aspects of applied behaviorism: education, corrections, treatment of the mentally ill and retarded, chemical dependency, and the like.

C. PASTORAL CARE AND COUNSELING

As Huckaby observed in his essay, one would expect that the pastoral care and counseling work of the priest, minister, or rabbi might be the area of institutional religious life where behavior modification would have the greatest impact. But that has not been the case. Aside from a very few references in recent pastoral counseling text-books to the kinds of behavior therapy which the minister should know about, there is very little literature suggesting any direct appropriation and use. There is one essay by Rickey L. George and E. Richard Dustin on "The Minister as a Behavioral Counselor," in *Pastoral Psychology* for December, 1970. The authors advocate behavioral methods for the counseling minister because:

"... it is our belief that if the minister is to function effectively in bringing about the kinds of behavioral changes that will fulfill the needs of people who come to him, then it is essential that he see these behavioral changes as problems in learning."[18]

The authors argue that the minister ought to work more on specific behavior and less with attitudes, so that:

"... the client is better able to understand where he is going in the counseling process, as well as the specifics for getting there. ... many clients become discouraged and fail to return to counselors because they are unable to see the relationship between their experienced problems and the manner in which the counselor sets out to help them."[19]

The authors then proceed to identify four specific beneficial aspects of behavioral counseling for the minister. First, the minister is helped by viewing counseling from the standpoint of a behavioral scientist. This entails careful observation and focusing on behaviors, rather than speculating about the motives or the intentions of the client.

The second beneficial aspect of behavior modification for the minister noted by George and Dustin is that behavioral approaches make the minister more of an equal with the client.

"Behavioral counselors recognize that change requires client's doing different actions. Resisting the rather easy 'one-upmanship' of reassurance, or some other one-way communication, the behavioral counselors seek a mutual level of communication.

"Negotiation is an example of two-way communication. During the negotiation phase of counseling, both the counselor and the client suggest and accept ideas. ... the negotiation phase terminates in a behavioral contract, in which the client and counselor agree to work toward certain concrete behavior changes."[20]

The third beneficial aspect of behavioral counseling for the minister is understanding the minister as an experimenter. This means that "... the counselor, like any experimenter, helps the client to try small behaviors in a safe environment, and gradually attempt harder, more complex changes."[21]

And, finally, George and Dustin identify the strength of the minister's reinforcements as the fourth beneficial aspect of behavioral counseling. "The minister, more than any other professional, must be aware of the extent to which he is a potent source of reinforcement."[22] Such reinforcements include the positive comments which the minister makes about the progress of client in counseling, and the way in which the minister traditionally serves as a model human figure in the religious community and in the larger society.

In this very brief but provocative article, George and Dustin have identified specific approaches in counseling which are clearly based on behavior modification, and have suggested ways for the minister to use them. Dr. George has published another article of the same sort, "Behavioral Counseling for the Minister."[23] Here he argues that the behavioral approach will help the minister be more efficient and effective because of the careful planning involved, which help eliminate non-selective reinforcement. As in the previous article, he emphasizes the importance of the minister's verbal and social reinforcements, and developing a mutually acceptable behavioral contract.

In all of the extensive literature on modern pastoral counseling, it is apalling that these are the only two articles (along with
Huckaby's) which suggest any possible usefulness of behavior modification.

In behavior modification books and journals, there are many
suggestive reports on individual counseling, marriage counseling
and family counseling which appear to lend themselves, with appropriate training and supervision, to the pastoral work of the minister.
I cite just two examples from this kind of literature.

Azrin, Naster and Jones have published an article on "Reciprocity
Counseling: A Rapid Learning-Procedure for Marital Counseling," in
the Journal, *Behavior Research and Therapy,* for 1973. The authors
describe marriage as a contractual relationship in which two individuals agree to marry when each expects "more reinforcement from
the married than the unmarried state."[24] Maritial difficulty is
defined as the situation in which one or both of the marriage partners
conclude that marriage has become less reinforcing than the unmarried
state.

The counseling method which the authors have developed and
tested is summarized as follows, "... the suggested method of assuring
marital reinforcers for oneself is to reinforce the spouse for providing them."[25]

The major part of the article describes a research project in
which couples were instructed to get what they need from their
spouses by reinforcing the spouse when these needs were met. In
other words, if Jack is reinforced by chocolate cream pie, and Jill
is reinforced by a dozen red roses, Jack can maintain or increase
the servings of pie by giving her red roses whenever pie is served.
The researchers found that such methods could be easily taught,
with rapid improvements in the marital situation on the basis of
few sessions of training.

> "The approach does not attempt to teach the client
> principles of reinforcement. Indeed, the instruc-
> tions to the clients scrupulously avoided technical
> terms such as reinforcement, extinction, time-out
> and instead used more common lay terms, such as
> happiness, satisfaction, frustration, motivation,
> desire and appreciation."[26]

Clergy might be put off by what appears to be a system for
barter or manipulation in marriage. But if marriage must be more
than a mutual arrangement for need satisfaction, as certainly any
religious understanding of marriage would insist, still it may be
worth checking to see if the relationship is breaking down simply

because these exchanges are out of balance, and trying to remedy that breakdown, rather than falling back on religious teachings about marital commitment and the prohibition of the divorce, or deciding that separation or divorce are the only alternatives.

The authors of this article do not state whether they regard such reciprocity counseling as requiring a certain kind or level of training on the part of the therapist, but one would suppose that just as there are many institutes and workshops today for the clergy and other counseling professionals in Adlerian or Gestalt or trans-actional therapies, similar behavioral workshops might be developed.

Another example of applied behavior modification which might lend itself to the work of the minister in pastoral care and counseling appears in an essay entitled, "A Behavioral Revolution in Community Mental Health," by McDonald, Hedberg and Campbell, in the *Community Mental Health Journal* for the summer of 1974. In this essay, the authors identify three fundamentally different kinds of interventions in personal and community problems. First, there is the role of the consultant-therapist, who deals primarily with clients or patients, those who have identified themselves as having diffi-culties needing aid, or those who have been identified by the courts or some other agency of society as requiring some kind of therapeutic intervention. Secondly, there is the model of the consultant-educator, in which there is a brokering of resources for individuals or groups as they find themselves needing something which they cannot locate on their own but which the consultant-educator can provide. The third kind of intervention or model is that of the consultant who is a systems-engineer, someone who understands how the entire social system functions, where and how the key decisions are made regarding the way in which the social system is to work, and who knows how "... to systematically use the natural community reinforcers for the strengthening of community systems."[27]

If we can translate into more common language, it would seem that the priest, minister or rabbi is in an excellent position to act in these three ways. The minister is a leader in a local system (church), is a leader in the larger social system of the neighborhood or city or region in which the minister works. At given points the minister will function in all three ways, as a therapist, as an educator, and as a "systems-engineer." In other words, there is a time to heal, there is a time to educate, but there is also a time to analyze and mobilize by bringing a systems and behavioral learning analysis to bear on what is happening. That should help a church or community to see that the problems of certain people do not reflect their own failings or weaknesses as individuals, but reflect something about the character of the community system which is reinforcing the behavior which continues to be destructive to the individual and the community.

These two examples of the hundreds of articles of this kind, which appear in the literature of behavior modification therapy and and programs, suggest ways in which the primary training of persons for religious professional leadership and the continuing education of the clergy might be significantly strengthened and enhanced by behavioral approaches. I do not know of any places where such training is currently being offered or projected. If the behavioral therapies become as widely used as seems likely, clergy and other professionals will be climbing on the bandwagon. It is important that the development of such a network or system for training clergy in behavioral counseling be done collaboratively, between those engaged in the teaching and practice of behavior modification and those engaged in the teaching and practice of pastoral care and counseling. Otherwise, we will endure another fad in which "the latest therapy" is uncritically heralded as the solution to all those tough human problems which confront the minister day after day.

Having judged the impact of behavior modification therapies on pastoral counseling to be negligible, I should add that there is a generalized behavioral drift in pastoral counseling from other sources. The use of enacted vignettes in Gestalt therapy and in Psychodrama, in which the client and the therapist play a scene involving physical activity, adds behavioral dimensions, taking counseling beyond conversation. There is also behavioral influence in the increasingly common practice of forming explicit contracts regarding what the client hopes to be able to achieve, what the counselor can promise to provide, and the expected practice periods between counseling sessions.

It may be that behavior modification will be appropriated in pastoral care and counseling in this indirect way rather than by means of specific behavioral techniques. Most clergy will probably never be trained in or find it appropriate to use all the techniques currently employed in the practice of psychiatry and psychotherapy by the major schools of behavioral therapy. Aversive methods of counter-conditioning would seem out of place in the work of the minister, except as the minister might contract with a parishioner or family to provide certain kinds of acceptable negative reinforcement when behaviors warranting them are exhibited. It does not seem likely or desirable that members of the clergy will some day be opening shop on their own as behavior modification counselors, as happens nowadays when ministers become full-time marriage and family counselors.

But it still seems to me that our current efforts in educating the clergy as counselors are seriously defective in failing to teach behavioral techniques which could appropriately be used by the pastoral counselor, and which might indeed the counselor's effectiveness with many difficult problems.

D. RELIGIOUS EDUCATION

As Huckaby noted in the initial essay considered in this chapter, religious education has apparently taken as little note of behavior modification as has pastoral care and counseling. In an essay by John L. Elias, "B. F. Skinner and Religious Education," in *Religious Education*, for September and October of 1974, this same observation is made: "B. F. Skinner has been virtually ignored by religious educators."[28]

Like Novak, Elias remarks on the similarity between Skinner and a certain kind of theology. "Has the extreme view that man is controlled by divine grace (which is external to man) influence his [Skinner's] view of man being completely controlled by an environment (which is external to man)?"[29]

Elias suggests that not all of religious education, however, is neglecting the behavioral approach. He notes that there is an approach to religious education being developed by James Lee at places like St. Louis University and University of Notre Dame which "is obviously influenced by Skinnerian ideas. But it also attempts to maintain the traditional image of man as a free and responsible person.

"... It rejects the classical conditioning of Pavlov but appears favorable to the operant conditioning of Skinner.

"Lee and others who espoused the social science approach make no reference to the works of Skinner, though I contend that they are greatly influenced by his particular brand of behaviorism."[30]

Elias takes up the question of the way in which one can critically appropriate Skinner's ideas without having to accept all of his environmental determinism and he suggests that "... the real value for the religious educator in reflecting upon Skinner's behavioristic interpretation of religious beliefs comes from the focusing of attention upon religious teaching as translated into behavior,"[31]

Elias poses Ivan Illich against B. F. Skinner as examples of Utopian totalists.

"Illich like Skinner is a totalist in his strong adherence to human freedom. He opposes the behavioral controls advocated by a Skinner. His analysis of social reality is more profound than

163

Skinner's but his knowledge of human behavior appears rather naive along side of Skinner's extended psychological investigations. Both Illich and Skinner buttress their Utopian thinking with apocalyptic visions of a coming catastrophe unless their warnings are heeded. Both have taken up the mantle of the prophet of doom and hope."[32]

In spite of the generally accurate assessment by both Huckaby and Elias that the literature of religious education has paid little attention to behaviorism and the work of B. F. Skinner, I believe the influence of behaviorism is also evident in the way in which religious education materials and methods reflect trends in the field of educational methods, as taught in our colleges and universities. The concern to provide positively reinforcing educational environments and materials, the attempts to target specific learning behaviors which are expected as outcomes of the teaching and learning process, all represent a behavioral orientation (and jargon!) in the discipline which is becoming evident in religious education as well as in public schools.

Another example of a way in which behavioral methods might be applied to religious education programs is suggested by an article on "Training Parents as Behavior Therapists: A Review", by Berkowitz and Graziano in *Behavior Research and Therapy*, volume 10, 1972. Their article summarizes treatment programs which have been designed to assist parents in dealing with problem behaviors in their children.

"... it is not the task of the therapist to assume the full burden of treatment and in the process allow the parents to relinquish their responsibility but it is the therapist's task to help the parent directly to be more effective in carrying out a parent's moral, ethical and legal obligation to care for the child."[33]

The article by Berkowitz and Graziano summarizes research which has been done with "respondent" training for parents, especially in treating bed-wetting problems. They summarize their findings in this way:

"... respondent principles have been used to teach parents to bring about the decrement of maladaptive behavior and for the establishment of new behavior.... Parents can be trained to apply respondent-based techniques to a variety of behavior. Such training appears to be a relatively uncomplicated task which may yield high clinical returns."[34]

The authors also report that with really serious family problems, an hour or two of therapy a week with the trained counselors simply does not do the job unless the parents are trained to respond in a therapeutic way throughout each day in all of the interactions of family members.

This kind of article suggests ways in which religious institutions offering family life or parental guidance programs could be enriched with behavioral approaches. Even if the clergy are not trained in behavior modification, it would still be possible for local churches or clusters of churches to offer family life or parental education programs in which behavior therapists from private practice or colleges and universities could be engaged to teach. That might also encourage the kind of dialogue which I have been advocating in this book.

The final example of applied behavior modification in religious education is contained in the second essay by Richard C. Schlotman, noted earlier. Schlotman describes a youth fellowship program in a suburban church, where a dynamic young man who was serving as a lay leader had encouraged a style of youth fellowship life which was causing concern among parents, adult leaders, and the minister. They feared that the young people were overemphasizing the personal and private dimension of religious enthusiasm to the neglect of the social dimension. With the consent of adult leaders, but not the young people, Schlotman trained the enthusiastic young lay leader in a few simple techniques of behavior modification so that he might give his familiar positive reinforcements ("Praise the Lord," "yes, Jesus," a smile or hug) to the kinds of religious expressions which would be more acceptable to their parents and to the adult leaders of the congregation. The young lay leader had to be trained to recognize and respond to those "better" expressions instead of the ones which he was more naturally inclined to reinforce. Within a short period of time, there was a marked increase in the number of expressions by the young people which conveyed a concern for others, and the social dimension of faith, without a noticable loss in their enthusiasm or their loyalty to the young man who was serving as the lay leader. In due time, the opinions of parents and adult leaders were sought, and they were all much happier with the way in which the youth fellowship was going.

Schlotman's essay is the only one I could find in any of the literature in which such a clear and deliberate application of operant reinforcement was used in a church setting. Schlotman was primarily trying to demonstrate this thesis that behavior modification could be used to resolve the conflict he saw between form-dominant and dynamic-dominant church organizations. (The youth fellowship representing the dynamic-dominant type and the church leaders representing the form-dominant type). Schlotman concludes his argument this way:

"The new dynamic may be viewed in terms of the
operant behavior model. The channels will be
found where behavior is reinforced by satisfactory
internal and external rewards. It is not enough
to allow the new dynamism to find its own forms or
to be captured by those who are alert enough to use
it for their own purposes. Dynamic seeks forms,
whether these be shaped by dictators for selfish
ends or by others for meaningful living and human
enrichment. Either Christians have a way and can
specify it behaviorally or we don't. If we do, we
will develop and train the operant dynamics of our
times or be relevant to a new age."[35]

I certainly want to agree with Schlotman that the churches must
be much more clear and deliberate about their behavior-modifying
activities. My strenuous objection to the project which he reported
with the youth fellowship was the fact that the young people themselves were apparently never asked to consent to the behavior modification which was undertaken. This is a serious violation of the ethics
of behavior modification stated in the previous chapter. I am truly
surprised that so many people consented to engage in this project
without apparently even asking whether the young people should be
consulted regarding their own desire to modify their religious
behavior in the ways which the project designers thought desirable.

E. CONCLUSION AND SUMMARY

We have looked at nearly all the literature I could find which
discusses any possible appropriation of behavior modification in the
life of religious institutions. Again I am astonished by this neglect.
But I continue to hope that religious institutions will be enriched
by behavior modification in their tasks of theological reformulation,
social action, pastoral care and counseling, and religious education.
Theology and faith can be enlivened by disciplined attention to all
of the environmental ways in which human life is shaped and directed,
so that God's creative and grace-filled interventions will be better
understood. Ethical analysis and action can be enhanced by coming
to informed judgments about new methods of treatment and new programs
for modifying institutions and whole societies. The pastoral care
and counseling work of the priest, minister, or rabbi can be considerably strengthened by the addition of behavioral methods, without
losing the value of relationships of genuine love and caring. And
church education programs may become far more successful in specifying
the kinds of persons and institutions we want ourselves to be as
religious people, by using behavioral analysis and behavior modification methods.

It is too early to know whether these gains will be achieved. There is considerable resistence in the church circles in which I move toward any consideration of the behavioral approach. If we continue to neglect or reject behavior modification, we will lose an important opportunity to assist our society in thinking through the implications of this new technology, and we will just lose the many beneficial effects for the religious institution.

NOTES FOR CHAPTER V

[1] Phillip Huckaby, "Survey of the Response to Behavioral Psychology in Recent Religious Literature," *Journal of Pastoral Care*, XXXIX, No. 4, December, 1975, 263.

[2] *Ibid.*, 264.

[3] *Ibid.*

[4] *Ibid.*, 266.

[5] Russell C. Llewellyn, "A Second Look at B. F. Skinner," *Journal of Psychology and Theology*, I, 3, July, 1973, 6.

[6] Martin E. Seligman, *Helplessness: On Depression, Development and Death*. (San Francisco: W. H. Freeman, 1975).

[7] James H. Reynierse, "Behavior Therapy and Job's Recovery," *Journal of Psychology and Theology*, III, 3, Summer, 1975, 87.

[8] *Ibid.*, 92.

[9] Michael Novak, "Is He Really a Grand Inquisitor?" in *Beyond the Punitive Society*, ed. Harvey Wheelis. (San Francisco: W. H. Freeman and Company, 1973), 231.

[10] *Ibid.*, 233.

[11] *Ibid.*

[12] *Ibid.*, 235.

[13] *Ibid.*, 236.

[14] *Ibid.*, 237.

[15]*Ibid.*, 246.

[16]Richard C. Schlotman, "Theology and Behavior Modification," *The Chicago Theological Seminary Register*, vol. LXI, No. 5, September, 1971, 4.

[17]*Ibid.*, 17.

[18]Rickey L. George and E. Richard Dustin, "The Minister as a Behavioral Counselor," *Pastoral Psychology*, Vol. 21, No. 209, December, 1970, 16.

[19]*Ibid.*

[20]*Ibid.*, 17.

[21]*Ibid.*, 18.

[22]*Ibid.*

[23]Rickey L. George, "Behavioral Counseling for the Minister," *Journal of Pastoral Counseling*, Vol. 7, No. 2, 1972-73, 42-47.

[24]Nathan H. Azrin, Barry J. Naster and Robert Jones. "Reciprocity Counseling: A Rapid Learning - Based Procedure for Marital Counseling," *Behaviour Research and Therapy*, 1973, Vol. 11, 366.

[25]*Ibid.*, 367.

[26]*Ibid.*, 381.

[27]K. R. MacDonald, A. G. Hedberg, L. M. Campbell, "A Behavioral Revolution in Community Mental Health," *Community Mental Health*, x, e, Summer, 1974, 230.

[28]John L. Elias, "B. F. Skinner and Religious Education," *Religious Education*, LXIX, No. 5, September - October, 1974, 558.

[29]*Ibid.*, 560.

[30]*Ibid.*, 563.

[31]*Ibid.*

[32]*Ibid.*, 565-566.

[33]Barbara P. Berkowitz and Anthony M. Graziano, "Training Parents as Behavior Therapists: A Review," *Behavior Research and Therapy*, Vol. 10, 1972, 299.

[34]*Ibid.*, 301.

[35]Schlotman, *Loc. cit.*, 37.

INDEX

INDEX

Cornell University - 10
constitutional guarantee of rights - 2, 3, 118-119, 120, 126, 136
counter-control - 32-24, 26, 93-94, 103, 110, 113, 117, 120
Craighead - 22, 26, 35-36

D'Angelo, Edward - 38, 45
Darwin, Charles - 31, 90
Davis, William H. - 46
death of God theologians - 153
Delgado, Jose - 3-4
determinism - definition of - 38; difference from fatalism - 38;
     emotional or spiritual character - 39; soft and hard - 38-39, 45, 99
Descartes, Renee - 17
desensitization, systematic - 8, 24-25, 134, 152
     originator of - 24
DiCaprio - 25
"Dilemma of Determinism, The" - 38, 39
Dustin, E. Richard - 158-159

Edwards, Jonathan - 64-66, 67, 75, 76
Elementary School Journal, The - 102
electrode implants - 24
Elias, John L. - 163-164
Enlightenment, the - 78
Erasmus - 60
Ethics of Manipulation - 122

Farrar, Austin - 46-47
Feigl, Herbert - 38, 41-44, 46, 47, 48, 52
Frances, Evan - 11
Frankl, Viktor - 70
Franklin, R. L. - 48, 64
Free-Will and Determinism - 48
Free-Will Question, The - 46
Freedom of the Will, The - 46
Freud, Sigmund - 19, 149, 150-151
From Pigeons to People - 103-104

Gaylin, Willard - 100-101
Ghost in The Machine, The - 97-98
George, Rickey, L. - 158-159
Gestalt therapy - 149, 161, 162
Gochros, Harvey L. - 102
Goffman, Erving - 114, 119
Goldiamond, Israel - 118-121
Graziano, Anthony M. - 164-165
Gregory of Nyssa - 54-55, 63, 75, 77

171

INDEX

INDEX

INDEX

Clyde J. Steckel was born and reared in Anderson, Indiana, and educated at Butler University (B.A.), Chicago Theological Seminary (B.D.), and the University of Chicago (M.A., Ph.D). In the Religion and Personality program at the University of Chicago he studied with Seward Hiltner, Granger Westberg, Carl Rogers and Charles Stinnette. He is an ordained minister in the United Church of Christ, and has served parish ministries in Chandlerville and Waverly, Illinois, as well as Protestant Chaplain of the Illinois Children's Hospital School in Chicago, Chaplain and Assistant Professor of Religion at Illinois College in Jacksonville, Illinois, and University Pastor for United Ministries in Higher Education at the University of Minnesota. Since 1970 he has been on the faculty of United Theological Seminary of the Twin Cities, where he is Professor of Theology and Psychology and Director of the M.Div. program. He has also served as Director of the D.Min. program of the Minnesota Consortium of Theological Faculties.

His hobbies include music, painting, jogging, racquetball and camping.

He is married to Eleanor Todd Steckel, and they have three sons: James, of Phoenix, Arizona, and David and Mark of Minneapolis.